HANGING
by a
Thread

The Erosion of the Golden Rule In America

BUSINESS

DAVID M.
Armstrong

Hanging By A Thread: The Erosion of the Golden Rule in America
by David M. Armstrong
Copyright © 2008 by David M. Armstrong
All Rights Reserved.
ISBN: 1-59755-178-3

Published by: ADVANTAGE BOOKS™
                 www.advbookstore.com

Scripture quotations marked "NIV" are taken from the HOLY BIBLE, NEW INTERNATIONAL VERSION®. NIV®. Copyright © 1973, 1978, 1984 by International Bible Society. Used by permission of Zondervan. All rights reserved.

Scripture quotations marked "NKJV™" are taken from the New King James Version®. Copyright © 1982 by Thomas Nelson, Inc. Used by permission. All rights reserved.

Library of Congress Control Number: 2008941513

Cover design by Pat Theriault

First Printing: December 2008
08 09 10 11 12 13 14   10 9 8 7 6 5 4 3 2 1
Printed in the United States of America

Special Dedication

To my father, Merrill "Gus" Armstrong:

For all the time spent with me on the importance of core values and ethics within the workplace. Dad always said, "I don't want to be the biggest company, I want to be the best company." We promise to provide enjoyable experiences that fulfill Dad's vision. Thanks Dad.

David Armstrong

Table of Contents

Foreword

In a world that is laden with headlines citing various business executives for unethical behavior, David Armstrong has chosen to take a vastly different path when it comes to integrity – heading up a global corporate culture that is defined by following the Golden Rule. In fact, the company motto at Armstrong International is simply put into this historical phrase – "Do unto others as you would have them do unto you."

In this powerful book, you will learn how David Armstrong has led a successful company through his many key examples that smack of integrity -- through his everyday ethical leadership style that includes the telling of vital stories which showcase the very premise of what his company stands for.

David Armstrong directs a corporate culture that is indeed unique. How about company core values that place faith in God first; family, second; and your job last? Yes, believe it or not, this is promoted and posted virtually everywhere within the organization. This is what makes David Armstrong and the company that he leads so unique. It's not your typical company and David Armstrong is no typical CEO – particularly when so many corporate scandals fill the headlines today. It's all quite refreshing to see.

In some of my previous writings, I have cited that "Integrity is King." How true that phrase is and most fitting as it relates to David Armstrong. A person of integrity is honest and upright. His soul is not divided or compartmentalized. As the Bible tells us, "He who walks with integrity walks securely, but he who perverts his ways will become known" (Prov. 10:9, NKJV).

This book is all about integrity in the workplace and how David Armstrong exemplifies this as a leader. Armstrong does not abandon his values or principles under pressure.

Times of adversity and temptation are precisely when values and principles matter most. David Armstrong keeps his promises and fulfills his obligations. And, it's also safe to say that Armstrong Is a man who maintains his honor even when it is costly to do so.

So, if you wish to learn more about how to be a successful leader without selling your soul to do so, read on ... and, be prepared to gain a very valuable lesson in just how to lead a successful company through the eyes of David Armstrong.

Pat Williams
Senior Vice President
Orlando Magic

Pat Williams has written nearly 40 motivational books. He's also one of America's top motivational speakers, and has been a featured speaker at two Billy Graham Crusades. He's also addressed employees from many of the Fortune 500 companies. Pat's website is: www.patwilliamsmotivate.com

Introduction

Becoming a Force for Good

Too proud to cry and too overcome to speak, Fred Kemp just nodded and extended a leathery, work-roughened hand. And so in that forgotten five-second exchange between two simple men of honor, a promise was made. Forget business and profits. Let go of practicality and good business sense. This covenant had nothing to do with any of them. But it had everything to do with human dignity, the sanctity of a pledge freely given and the best of which men are capable.

Armstrong International's promise to Fred Kemp, an aging former employee, speaks more eloquently than all of our leaders put together. It's more impressive than our product innovations, foreign locations, record-setting years and 108 years of business. And it's more powerful than the combined might of every computer we own. It has been said that nothing binds like promises kept, and nothing divides like promises broken. This is a story, actually many stories, about people, prayers, partnerships and the profound power of promises kept.

Yes, you'll learn about our promise to Fred Kemp, but later. First things first. To understand what I'm trying to accomplish as CEO of Armstrong International, Inc., you need a few basics about our company. Armstrong is a faith-based business. Period. No debates, no apologies and no second-guessing. I have faith in God, family and job, in that order. I would like to believe that all our employees do likewise. But they don't.

That's okay—as long as they understand and accept that the owners and leaders of Armstrong International do. They must further understand that we run the company in a way that mirrors that priority of faith. No, you don't have to be a Christian to thrive at Armstrong. But you must have faith. You must devote yourself to what we believe in and the principles on which we stand. Surviving and thriving at Armstrong depends on it.

The second fundamental you must understand is that the motto of Armstrong International is, "Do unto others as you would have them do unto you." Yup. The Golden Rule.

In addition to faith in God, family and your job (in that order), our core values are Honesty, Fairness, Respect, Trust, Loyalty, Dignity, Hard Work, Kindness and Fearlessness.

Oh, it's okay. Go ahead and ask. You wouldn't be the first. Here let me do it for you. Most of the time the question goes something like this: *"Isn't that a little over the top? A little . . . naïve? This is business, after all."*

Nope. Any other questions?

Finally, if the company conducts itself according to the dictates of an unwavering faith in God, family and job and if we observe the Golden Rule in our dealings with all those we encounter, it follows that doing business with Armstrong will be an enjoyable experience. That is our goal. And employees must understand that we will gauge their conduct—with management, associates, customers, business partners and suppliers—against that yardstick. No exceptions.

Lead Horse in a Company-wide Harness

Of my many jobs as CEO of Armstrong International, none is more important than shaping and nurturing our corporate culture. None. We have systems and procedures for running the business. And lots of talented people who have been taught to manage themselves. But tending to our corporate culture is the one job I cannot pass off to others. Identifying and nurturing new leaders at every level and in every corner of our business is a job I must not delegate. These are two of the biggest bucks that stop here. And rightly so.

I believe it is the CEO's job to personify the company's vision, to the extent that is possible. I need to live it. Breathe it. And act as if our very existence depends on it because, in the end, it does.

To thrive, Armstrong International must be a group of people all pulling in the same harness. All linked and synergized by a common belief in our ability to succeed and make a difference. We must have a strong sense of identity. While we may have many views, a single vision should guide us. And regarding the things that matter most (remember the Golden Rule), we must be one.

It has been said that nothing binds like promises kept, and nothing divides like promises broken.

I must keep the soil fertile and the weeds whacked. Because unless I create an *environment* suitable for growing, the crop will never mature. Grow, maybe. But not mature and reach full potential. And what are we growing? Human capital empowered and set free to become what their gifts make possible.

I want an environment where employees feel valued and important. I want them driven and inspired by our trust in them. Self-control is always the best control whether you're talking about quality control, arriving to work on time (or arriving at all) or self-inspection. We don't have time clocks, yet few come late. We believe in self-inspection, and our scrap rate is 0.4 percent. The point? Give people responsibility for their actions, and they will invariably do the right thing.

The erosion of our culture is the greatest threat to Armstrong. That's worth repeating: *The erosion of our culture is the greatest threat to Armstrong.* That's exactly why I spend so much time nurturing our culture. I believe that in the right environment, leaders will self-select, step forward and take advantage of an opportunity to improvise when the job requires it. Better yet, such an environment is a catalyst for innovation, outreach and experimentation—creativity. For Armstrong's future leaders, it sets inhibitions free and gives wings to imagination. And they, the leaders five or ten years down the road, are exactly the ones I seek.

Another question?

I'll bet I've heard this one too, but go ahead.

Okay, okay. I get it. But isn't it risky business to create the potential for a free-for-all? When does self-management give way to self-interest?

If employees are committed to our common belief, they simply cannot be driven by self-interest. They have to be one or the other. And making the wrong choice is a one-way ticket out. Besides, there is very little potential for chaos or a free-for-all. First, human nature suggests that most employees simply won't rock the boat, even if given the chance—and assured that a little rocking is a good thing. For most, a feeling of security, borne of predictability, usually overpowers whatever urges to innovate might bubble to the surface. Another reason is that I have given every Armstrong employee a sense of how to behave—even in an environment where there are few rules. It is a foolproof way of checking to see if they are in sync with the Armstrong brand. It's called the Seven Ss. Now be clear—these are business strategies for success, not core values.

1) Swiftest
2) Simplest
3) Smallest
4) Spirit of Intrapreneurship*
5) Surprises
6) Storytelling
7) Smiles

(*"Intra" being within or inside. So be an entrepreneur within your own department, group, function, etc.)

If employees promote, implement and enforce these seven strategies, they really can't be very far afield. Later, we'll look at stories exemplifying these characteristics. But for now, suffice it to say that all of these features describe an entrepreneur or entrepreneurship.

Soooo . . . you want every employee to act like an entrepreneur?

Bingo. Not only act like one, but eat, sleep and live as an entrepreneur. Why? I believe these seven traits embody success. Now, believe me, not every successful company trots out these guidelines and chants them in <u>unison</u>. Probably none do. Not even Armstrong does that. But we do try very hard to weave them into the fabric of our corporate culture and integrate them into the course of daily business. I believe the Seven Ss are a recipe for success and that industry leaders, with modifications, of course, all employ them in one way or another.

Nothing is more important than cultivating our culture and enriching the soil in which it grows. The stakes are high because we are only a generation away from losing the simple truths which have guided Armstrong these four generations. To be what author Arie de Geus calls "The Living Company," I must do my job at this critical point in our company's history to make sure that Armstrong

- Remains alert and sensitive to surrounding circumstances. We must accelerate our rate of learning by sharing ideas with each other.

- Knits a strong sense of identity and community. Some call it a family atmosphere. A vision is needed, and we have one: *Generations of global customers, employees, partners, neighbors and stockholders will have many*

enjoyable experiences *when dealing with Armstrong International*. We also need a mission: *Armstrong is the simplest company for you to do business with*. And finally to protect and preserve this community we need strategies that are *timeless*. We call these the Seven Ss: *Swiftest, Simplest, Smallest, Spirit of Intrapreneurship, Surprises, Storytelling, and Smiles.* And… lets not forget those core values mentioned earlier.

- Is conservative in finances. Cash is king and always will be. Cash gives Armstrong International independence and flexibility. It allows us to survive during difficult times and invest in good times.

- Remains tolerant of experiments, demos and prototyping and yes . . . failures. The fear of risk-taking, demos and prototyping are the enemies of learning. Armstrong must remain impatient, fearless, nimble and open-minded. Be willing to experiment. Innovators play with prototypes. This is where new products and services come from and thus new markets that reinvent Armstrong International so it lives century after century.

I am keenly aware of my role as the living link between the founders and the future. Armstrong International is what it is today because three generations of Armstrongs before me always chose to do what was right; for people, then business. You'll learn about those choices through the stories you'll be reading. And you'll see how making the same simple choices more than a century later continues to separate Armstrong International from the business norm.

While my namesakes may not have packaged their business beliefs as the Seven S strategies, the principles behind them were identical. So to give you a better understanding of the origins of what it is I'm bound (and proud) to protect, I need to broaden your view. For a better grasp of the principle-centered leadership of my predecessors you'll be reading about later, it's helpful to know how it all began.

Spokes and "Dibbles"

On October 17, 1911, The Philadelphia Athletics won game 3 of the World Series against the New York Giants by a score of 3 to 2. Although the world took less note of it, the U.S. Patent Office also issued a patent for an obscure device, the Inverted Bucket Steam Trap, on the same date.

It wasn't the first patent for the fledgling enterprise first known as the Armstrong-Durst Machine Works of Chicago formed by James William Armstrong, Phillip E. Durst, Charles Smith and John Adam Armstrong. The company entered into an exclusive licensing agreement with John Kennedy and became owners of his patent for a machine for swaging bicycle spokes in 1899. They also held a patent issued in 1906 for a mold used to form cement fence posts and had applied for a patent on the Dodge Potato Digger.

In its first years, the firm billed itself as *"Manufacturers of Special Machinery,"* wrote Lawrence (Armey) Armstrong. Early products were ". . . mostly things that were new inventions—whenever anyone wanted comparatively few items." These "things" included a harness bit designed to ease the strain on a horse's mouth, controls for furnace drafts, a machine which filled grain sacks and sewed them shut and a machine for printing and cutting milk bottle caps. Other product offerings included railway hand cars, "dibbles" (steel implements used to form the hole for setting strawberry plants in the ground) and a strawberry plant digger, an adaptation of the earlier potato digger.

At the turn of century, the firm had cast about for a location closer to their sources of supply and away from the high rents of the city. Company officials "found" Three Rivers, Michigan, through an ad placed by the Three Rivers Improvement Association. The civic group agreed to provide land and a building. In turn, the company agreed to employ at least 15 people for a period of five years, after which it would receive title to the land and building. So it was that a lot on the southwest corner of Maple and Bennett Streets became headquarters of the new Armstrong Machine Works. (The name was changed after the move to Three Rivers.)

Many small industries in the early 1900's used a single pot-bellied stove in the middle of a central room for heat. Those working any distance from the stove returned from time to time for warmth and the companionship of others clustered around it. The pot-bellied stove became the center of interest in most plants. Men held discussions around it, made decisions, and often drove their points home by illustrating them with white chalk on the smooth black sides of the stove.

One day in 1910, Adam Armstrong was warming himself near the black stove in the D&A Post Mold Company talking to Otto Arner, a former steamfitter. Otto had an idea for inverting the bucket in a steam trap so it would not air-bind, a shortcoming common to every float and bucket trap then on the market. To illustrate his point, Otto sketched his idea on the side of the stove...

Adam Armstrong researched the idea, made improvements and with Otto Arner's agreement patented the Inverted Bucket Steam Trap. On the advice of an executive at *Power Plant Engineering*, the company marketed the new product as the "Armstrong Steam Trap" . . . so the customer would have only one name to remember. Today the Armstrong name is synonymous throughout the world with steam system efficiency and smart steam trapping practices.

Within these pages you'll learn about my family's company and our business. You'll discover how I have earned my place among the Armstrongs who came before me to build a force for good. And if you're willing, I'll show you how to grow not just a business, but a business built on love, trust and faith that will live forever.

David Armstrong

Chapter One

Let Me Tell You a Story...

Only with divine intervention did I discover the rich mother lode of story material that surrounds us. One Sunday I was listening to Reverend Dr. Dale Kent explain the parable of the talents: God gives everyone a talent, and He expects each of us to use it to the best of our ability. As I was nodding in agreement, I noticed an amazing by-product of that familiar story—*interest*. People who had been nodding off or daydreaming were suddenly attentive. Even though they knew the story and its ending, still they listened. In a flash, I understood *that people like stories and will listen to them.* I realized right then and there that "Let me tell you a story..." could be an irresistible invitation.

What a great way of communicating, I thought. Why can't we use storytelling in our company, Armstrong International, Inc.? I loved the idea of telling a story to get a point across. People have always done it. Storytelling pre-dates written languages. Cave men told stories recapping their hunting triumphs by painting pictures on cave walls. Native Americans told stories to pass along their culture from one generation to the next. Mountain folks told stories to entertain family and friends. Jesus was a master storyteller. The fact that hundreds of millions of people around the globe still read His stories and parables speaks volumes about the endurance of stories and storytelling. Right there in church, I decided we would tell stories in our company. We'd tell stories about our goals and objectives. We would use stories to explain our core values and share our vision of the future. We'd even celebrate our victories with stories.

I started telling stories at Armstrong immediately and, as I had hoped, storytelling turned out to be an amazingly effective form of communication. Rules, either in policy manuals or on signs, can be inhibiting. But the morals in stories are invariably inviting, fun and inspiring. Thanks to storytelling, our people have a very clear understanding of what Armstrong stands for. And what we won't stand for.

Why I Tell Stories.

I tell stories because doing so makes me a more effective leader and helps me accomplish my most important task—preserving the Armstrong culture. Through stories I have created an environment in which people are more receptive to change and new ideas. Stories of the culture in action help people recognize and understand what their role at Armstrong can and should be.

Stories extend the gift of friendship. Telling them is enjoyable and a treat for people who are waiting to hear what I have to say. They want to know how it all ends. They pay attention. And if you don't have attention, you won't be successful with one of a leader's most challenging jobs—communication. As leaders, we must communicate. And that's hard to do if nobody's listening.

My self-imposed need to tell stories helps me to pay attention, too. I stay alert to where a story may be told or found. And storytelling helps me establish an agenda when I am talking with people. I used to stop by an office and say, "What's the stupidest policy at Armstrong?" Or I'd ask something like, "Are you having fun?" or "What can we do faster?" Then I'd wait for the answer and move on, thinking I had communicated.

Today, the Armstrong culture rests on storytelling. As a result, I am naturally led to go further. Since I'm constantly looking for fresh stories or scouting new places to tell old ones, I now find myself digging beneath the surface.

Through stories, I have created an environment in which people are more receptive to change and new ideas.

I tell stories because it's a great way to make—or underscore—a point. People turn off a lecture but turn on to stories. Storytelling means continuous reinforcement of the principles and attitudes I want employees to model. Besides, telling stories is one of the easiest and most acceptable ways of injecting passion into business.

Stories provide recognition and rewards for your people. People love to hear and read about people—especially themselves. Each time I mention an Armstrong employee in a story, that person receives a framed copy of the original story with a personal note from me. You'd be amazed at the number of people who have "their story" hanging in their office or by their machine. I've even found a few in their homes and once I spotted a framed story above the fireplace mantle. House decorations . . . proof that storytelling is great recognition.

Stories speak to all levels of experience. The most seasoned leader will enjoy a good story. So will the greenhorn! I have seen no evidence of a 40-year veteran or a two-year rookie being disenchanted with a story. Both would be wise to tell stories.

Stories will help you preserve and pass along corporate traditions. The stories a company tells show what it believes in, and the morals of these stories instruct people on how they should behave. Good stories are your company's best ambassadors.

Stories provide stability and comfort in times of change and uncertainty. Every day we deal with change. It is nice to know there is something that never changes: A story. Sure, the content may evolve, but the story itself and how it is told remains basically the same as it was in the time of Aristotle 2,000 years ago.

Stories may be your most informative teachers. At Armstrong, stories tell people how we do things. They tell people what may get them promoted—and what will certainly get them fired.

Stories empower every employee and encourage initiative. Stories provide guidelines, but getting the job done is up to the people themselves. Once they learn and internalize what we believe as a company, they largely manage themselves.

Stories can help you recruit. When we are interviewing people and hear the inevitable question about what our company is like, we hand them a storybook. Reactions to stories also help us evaluate how well a candidate may fit at Armstrong. We often give a story or two without morals to candidates we're thinking of hiring and ask them to give us the morals. Their answers go a long way toward determining whether we hire them.

Stories can help you sell a product or service. Potential customers want to know what kind of firm they are going to be doing business with if they buy Armstrong International products. Stories are the best way to share the value of our products and services. A water heater that can't scald you comes to life when it's in a story that you can personally relate to. If you've ever taken a shower in a hotel you know the water can suddenly get scalding hot without you touching the faucet. The pain of hot water hitting your back is not easily forgotten. Did you just remember a time that you had to jump out of the water to adjust the temperature so it was colder? The ending to this story is that the hotel needs an Armstrong Flo-Rite-Temp ™ Hot Water Heater. To learn more about this innovative product, read on. You're hooked, and it began with a story. Stories are best when they come from your own life experiences.

Stories are the lifeblood of Armstrong. And telling them is how we keep it coursing through the corporate body. Storytelling is inseparable from how we manage people (or encourage them to manage themselves). It plays a part in how we create new products and produce current ones. How we conduct business with partners, suppliers and customers. And it certainly looms prominently in our vision for the future of our business—and for the planet we all share. But if none of these things were true, I would still be preaching stories and storytelling. Why?

Stories are simple. You don't need an MBA, a college degree or even a high school diploma to tell stories—or to understand them. You've been telling and listening to stories since childhood. Telling stories is just as appropriate for doctors, lawyers and physicists as it is for plumbers, carpenters and drill press operators.

Stories are timeless. Unlike the latest management fads, storytelling is ageless. Stories stand the test of time. Don't believe me? Remember those stories Jesus told 2,000 years ago? What else is timeless in these days of constant change?

Stories are for all ages. So you're 93 and in your twilight years. So what? I'll bet you love to hear a good story. Or better yet—tell one. Be honest. You know you do. But you could also be 60 and at the end of your career, 45 in those peak years, or 22 and just getting started on your first job. I have never found a person—no matter what age—who didn't like a story.

Stories engage your memory. We can all remember a story from long ago told by Grandpa or another loved one. In business, most of the profound decisions are made emotionally, not rationally. A story brings out our emotions and therefore the right story may help us make a decision. We just need a nudge.

Stories are easy to retell. Most of us have trouble remembering the list of high tech features for our cell phones, video cameras, digital cameras, car navigation system, televisions and computers. The instruction manuals are hard to remember, but what if they were revealed in a story? Would we remember them better?

Stories are a mouthpiece of the world. I have visited many countries and have always found stories to be cherished and part of the culture at home – no matter where home is. That's right. People around the world tell their children bedtime stories just like we do. On my first trip to China the President of Kangsen Armstrong met me at the airport with books in hand. "Look, Mr. Armstrong, we have stories in China, too. I wanted you to have these books full of Chinese stories so you would better understand Chinese culture." I took a quick glance and recognized a story. "Wait a minute. This is an American story, isn't it?"

Telling stories is one of the easiest and most acceptable ways of injecting passion into business.

Stories are fun and memorable. People *like* stories. They listen to and connect with them. Which would you rather hear? "Now I'd like to review the highlights of our new XYZ procedures." or "Let me tell you a story..."

Every company has a rich heritage of stories that can innovate, lead, inspire and motivate your people while helping them solve the problems they face every day. Why not find your company's buried treasure and put it to work?

I ask you to approach storytelling in your company fearlessly. While I can share general guidelines about stories and storytelling (as I did in Chapter One of my first book, *Managing by Storying Around*), the fact of the matter is that you are going to—and should—develop your own storytelling style. Telling stories is a lot like telling jokes with style. Timing is important. If using a different tone of voice or improvising an accent will improve a story, give 'em a try. We're not talking about right or wrong here, only comfortable and uncomfortable. Adopt a style that fits and feels comfortable—one that links you to your audience and has the power to drill your point home. Know your audience and tailor your stories accordingly. After all, the whole point of storytelling is communicating, and you can't do that unless you're heard and understood. Before long, you will recognize the enormous power of stories to condition and cultivate your audience so they are receptive to your messages. Stories give people a way to think about and understand things that announcements, memos, e-mails, white papers and the like never could.

How I Tell Stories.

Go ahead and ask the question you've been waiting to ask. Why don't I help you: "but… David, I'm not any good at telling stories. I don't know how." I thought the same thing when I first got started, but you know what, it wasn't that difficult. Still let me give you a few secrets to put your mind at ease:

- Use a catchy title. It draws the reader into the story. Also, choose a title that helps you remember the story, so when you have 400 stories like I do; you can remember one if an employee ask you about the story titled, "Crayola Crayons." You guessed it – it's a story about crayons.

- "Once upon a time… ." Do you remember what you did the last time you heard these words? Chances are you looked up and listened intently to what was said. "Once upon a time" signaled that something interesting and meaningful was about to be told. What did that letter in the word "once" look like? Old French Script. Was the "O" larger than the other letters? Sure it was. This first letter informs the reader that they are about to embark on a story. Now here is one of my secrets. You can use any word, <u>not</u> just "Once," to start a story, but you must enlarge the first letter and use old French Script.

- Use employee names whenever possible. Most people want to see their names in print. It also helps identify the people you want other employees to talk to for guidance or as a role model.

- Use dialog between characters. And … remember, don't tell us how the character feels but use words that reveal it to us. "She was sad to hear that he died." You should not need to tell the reader this. Her actions should tell you. "She fumbled for a tissue to wipe the tears that wet her cheek."

- Morals are a must. Morals are the soul of storytelling. You want no doubt, confusion or gray areas for interpretation. Our goal is to clearly communicate as well as entertain. One moral is fine, two morals better but four morals are too many. Keep the morals focused on the same topic like quality. Don't have moral one on quality and moral two on service in the same story.

- Less is better. Resist the temptation to use adjectives and adverbs. And remember what Aristotle once said, "speak as the common man, think as a wise man." So, keep the vocabulary simple – may I suggest 6th grade reading level like our newspapers. Let what you have to say be more important than how you say it.

- Write only what you believe. Stories must be true if they are to be believed. Few companies have ever been destroyed because their employees and customers learned too much truth.

- You're on your way, oh … I almost forgot the most important thing. Keep your story short. Maybe two pages but hopefully one. Why, you ask? If your write more than a few pages you will need to create the characters, scenes, plots, and this is very difficult. We are business storytellers, not authors or screenwriters with a story to tell.

In each of the succeeding chapters, I will give you a glimpse into a given subject. As we move along now through the stories about Armstrong, you'll see that the general business landscape portrayed in the first few pages of each chapter is very different from the lay of the land at Armstrong. I believe we have been successful because God has blessed how we choose to do business by the Golden Rule and how we choose to treat our partners, customers and employees. Am I saying, "Do what we do, and you will be successful?" Of course not. First of all, that would be impossible. Your chemistry is different than ours. We are uniquely Armstrong just as you are uniquely _____. Fill in the blank. You can't be exactly like us any more than we can be exactly like you. Neither of us would want that anyway. The real power and potential comes from leveraging the *unique* assets of your company.

Since we all share an existence within the world at large, you know what that's like. So as a counterpoint to the "This is the world" part, appearing at the beginning of each chapter, I will give you a peek inside Armstrong at the end of each chapter. You are free to draw your own conclusions. Don't think of this as a cookbook to be followed to the letter. View it instead as a collection of easy-to-follow recipes for some really tasty dishes. Not all will be to your liking, but when you find some that are, give 'em a try.

Each story ends with a moral. Mind you, it may not be a universally understood truth as you might find with an Aesop fable. After all, these are business stories, so I've taken the liberty of sharing the business lesson from my point of view. In addition to that, I've added commentary and observations to give you more background for the story on our company.

Finally, at the end of each chapter, I've compiled a list titled, "Let's make a promise to…" with simple take-a-ways: key points about core values, globalization, urgency, creativity—whatever the subject—you can easily apply in any setting. "Let's make a promise to…" says just what you think it does. Take action and try to make the world of business a better place. Maybe this book will become a dog-eared companion, a constant source of recipes to nourish your company's culture. Or maybe it will be a volume you pull down a few times a year because you want something deliciously different for a special occasion. Either way, I hope you'll develop a taste for how Armstrong flavors the world of business. And it all begins with a story.

Chapter Two

The Untouchables

It was April of 1959 when the Desilu Playhouse aired a two-part pilot of a new show called the *The Untouchables* on CBS. The drama was based on the real-life exploits of gangbuster, Eliot Ness. Ness, an agent for the Treasury Department, was instrumental in toppling Chicago's legendary Al Capone in 1931. The new show took its inspiration from the famous crime fighter's autobiography. It was an instant hit with the public, and it became a regular series the following year.

The title sprang from the reputation of Ness and his men as incorruptible and from a description of them in a Chicago newspaper as "untouchables." Each week the series tagged along as Ness and his agents battled the worst of organized crime's bad boys. The facts tell a different story, but what's a little license in the name of entertainment, right? In real life, Ness dismantled the Untouchable squad after taking down Al Capone. He and his men had nothing to do with most of the cases celebrated in the series. But no matter, the name stuck. And to this day, untouchable is a word we reserve for someone or something that is just plain incorruptible. Anyone or anything that stands fast, firm and steady no matter what.

Few candidates for untouchable status have ever emerged from business, government or the world at large. Trouble started early in the Garden of Eden when Adam and Eve just couldn't get the hang of a simple act of obedience. They couldn't very well blame their shortcomings on the great vague culprit, "human nature," as we do nowadays, because they had the free will to sin or not sin. After they sinned by biting an apple, their offspring lost their parents' chance to choose good vs. evil and never sin. Later, their children did their part in moving humankind along the path from bad to worse. Cain slew Able, chalking up history's first recorded murder.

Untouchable is a word we reserve for someone or something that is just plain incorruptible.

Misdeeds, large and small, pepper the length and breadth of history. From our vantage point of time, the age-old tendencies of human beings to lie, cheat and steal lend color, texture and interest to the past. In fact, most of us relish reading about the crimes of yesteryear. And we like digging into how yesterday's dirty deeds besmirched the images of history's players and helped shape the course of historical events. Remember "Boss Tweed" and the Tammany Hall machine from your history lessons?

In the decades following the Civil War, they swindled millions from New York City. A few decades later, the Teapot Dome Scandal muscled its way onto history's stage.

Taking its name from a Wyoming rock formation resembling a teapot, the scandal was probably the worst of many to rock the administration of Warren G. Harding.

The Dome was on top of an important government oil reserve. Harding's buddy, Interior Secretary Albert Fall, was convicted of taking bribes from oil executives in exchange for the right to drill at Teapot Dome. The equation was simple. You give me cash and gifts, and I'll give you special favors (Read: illegal advantage.) It's a familiar story, and one that tempted men and women act out in endless variation every day around the globe.

Humankind makes a new batch of history every day, and ill deeds flavor much of it. Many of the recent examples of lying, cheating and stealing are of passing interest to us. A famous homemaking maven spends time in prison for insider trading. So what? Celebrities of every stripe play out their indiscretions in front of the world. Do we care? Maybe we're curious. Or sometimes amused. But seldom are we outraged or overwhelmed. Other than an occasional half-hearted condemnation of the moral and ethical drift of the world, we are not really *touched*. Sheer volume makes bad deeds commonplace. Repetition dulls our capacity to be upset. Because they have no direct connection to us, our loved ones and our lives, they end up in the oh-well category.

A review of just two Internet sites (http://www.pbs.org and http://washingtonpost.com) yielded the following list of misdeeds.

Read 'em and Weep.

2001

An energy giant with 20,000+ employees working around the globe fell apart, declaring Chapter 11 in December. Signs of trouble were apparent as early as July when the company announced that it would post a large quarterly loss. The next month, the new CEO—only a few months on the job—resigned. About the same time, the Securities and Exchange Commission (SEC) began investigating losses. October brought an announcement that the company would trim shareholder value by $1.2 billion. The axe then fell on the CFO, and officials accused him of various misdeeds to hide losses totaling millions. In November came an admission of overstating profits to the tune of $600 million since 1997. Market value fell like a stone, and the company's credit rating plunged, forcing an immediate payback on millions of debt. Bankruptcy and the loss of thousands of jobs came before Christmas.

2002

In January, a $22 billion communications biggie filed one of the five largest bankruptcies in U.S. corporate history. Years before hundreds of millions in fiber optics losses staggered the company; it sold more than $1 billion in stock. The founder and chairman pocketed in excess of $730 million. Employees reported shady bookkeeping practices, and the FBI and the SEC started poking into the possibility that the company deliberately inflated revenues.

Sheer volume makes bad deeds commonplace. Repetition dulls our capacity to be upset.

Employees of a highly respected accounting firm destroyed thousands of documents relating to a client under investigation by the SEC. Following an investigation by the Justice Department, the firm was indicted and later convicted of obstruction of justice.

A communications company widely known in the western United States announced it had "incorrectly" tallied more than $1 billion in sales. Word of this mistake came only a few weeks after a communications competitor admitted to misstating earnings to the tune of $3.9 billion—leading to the giant's bankruptcy, the largest in U. S. history.

The government handed down indictments to a former CEO for a variety of crimes, including conspiracy to commit securities fraud and wire fraud, securities fraud and conspiracy to commit perjury and to obstruct justice, perjury and bank fraud. Officials accused him of trying to sell securities he didn't own, forging a signature on a fake document and of attempting to dump shares he knew from inside information were about to plunge in value.

In 2002, the vortex surrounding the collapse of a crooked energy giant sucked in one of nation's most respected accounting firms. The Justice Department indicted the whole firm to the horrified disbelief of 85,000 loyal employees around the world. Since the firm was self-insured, wrenching questions arose immediately about whether already-scheduled surgeries and procedures would be covered. Parents of college-bound youngsters fretted. The suction even caught retirees because a collapse would wipe out their retirement benefits and health insurance.

Some of the firm's 28,000 U. S. employees staged rallies and public demonstrations. They picketed. They took out full-page newspaper ads, trying to state the company's position. Children of endangered employees carried some of the signs at the rallies. One read: "My dad needs his job." Another said, "My dad did nothing wrong."

All of this because someone (or several someone's) gave in, took a shortcut or looked the other way. All because once-trusted men and women forgot the ordinary man's definition of integrity: Do the right thing even when no one is looking. Jesus said it best: "Do unto others as you would have them do unto you."

2003

In February, the U. S. Attorney General charged former high-ranking officials of a major communications company with fraud for improperly reporting a transaction involving the Arizona School Facilities Board. Among the charges government officials handed down against four officials were securities fraud, wire fraud, making false statements and conspiracy. Up to $1 million in fines and possible prison time came with the allegations.

In April, nearly two years of investigations into alleged improprieties in Wall Street investment banking firms drew to a close with history-making penalties. The $1.4 billion levy was one of the largest ever handed down by securities regulators. Officials assigned each of the offending firms an independent monitor to make sure they followed the terms of the settlement. Another provision of the settlement ordered the firms to fund an $85 million investor-education program.

2004

July witnessed the unraveling of one of the nation's largest cable television companies. The founder of the company and his son, the former CFO, were found guilty of a number of charges. Among the allegations were charges that company officials had skimmed millions off the top to fund personal excesses. Prosecutors also charged that the company hid more than $2 billion in debt and misled investors about growth and profit. Legal experts noted the case as one of the worst examples of company executives robbing a public company for personal gain.

2005

In late April, news broke that a prominent investment firm had fired a highly touted Wall Street analyst after an internal probe surfaced questions about personal trading.

In literally a day's time, crime at the top can turn the existence of decent, hard-working people upside down and inside out.

Also, in April, the kingpins in a multinational tax shelter plan received a 20-year jail sentence. The leaders were also ordered to pay fines and restitution amounting to more than $200 million. Their scheme had more than 1,500 clients who paid upwards of $250,000 each to take part in the firm's plans to hide income and assets.

As Usual, the Innocent Suffer Most

It's hard to connect with distant events involving people we do not know. Life moves on. Tomorrow there will be fresh news, new problems and other worries. And so we pause, shake our head in brief empathy and move on with our own lives. We have created catch-all phrases used to respond to life occurrences we really don't understand. "Well, that's the way it goes;" "That's not fair;" "So much for luck;" or "That's Murphy's law—what can go wrong will go wrong." Sometimes we don't even get that far. "I dunno . . ." we say, shaking our head and leaving it at that.

But what happens when a business crime comes home to roost? For the thousands of innocent employees caught in these webs, it is the end of life as they know it. In literally a day's time, crime at the top can turn the existence of decent, hard-working people upside down and inside out. Forget that they committed no crime. No matter. Like a powerful tsunami rushing toward the quiet shores of innocent lives, the destruction doesn't stop to separate the innocent from the guilty.

People who work at Armstrong International, Inc. know that they can't check their sense of right and wrong at the door when they arrive. Morality is on the job 24 hours a day. We all deal with temptation around the clock every single day. A worker might be tempted to steal products from the factory. Or steal time. Or falsify an expense voucher. Or take office supplies home. The temptations never end. Nor does the tendency to rationalize it away with lame excuses: "The company can afford it. In fact, they'll never miss it." This thinking misses the point completely. Affordability has nothing to do with the basic black-and-white reality of truth. In the end, you did or you didn't. If you didn't, thanks for your honesty and for resisting the temptation we all share. If you did, good-bye and have a nice life.

Endangered employees staged rallies and public demonstrations. Their children carried signs that read, "My dad did nothing wrong."

All together now, "Armstrong will fire you for stealing." We'll do the same for lying. "Honesty," said Thomas Jefferson, "is the first chapter of the book of wisdom." If you tell the truth, you don't have to remember what you said. Lying is a slippery slope heading in only one direction. Most lies require little support lies to bolster the big lie. It's hard to remember which little lies belong to which big ones and how the shaky house of deceit all fits together. So just tell the truth—and give your memory a break.

Why have we seen such an upsurge in corporate wrongdoing in the recent past? There's a lot to read about business ethics, and some of the commentary concludes that there are none because the very phrase is a blatant contradiction of terms, a laughable oxymoron. Some point to runaway incentives and the pressures on top execs to increase shareholder value. Others wring their hands, trying to figure out if it's a few rotten apples or whole orchards gone bad. Or, have we just gotten better at catching the wrongdoers?

Workplace Ethics

According to data collected by the 2005 National Business Ethics Survey (NBES), more than half of American workers have observed at least one type of ethical misconduct in the workplace, a slight increase from 2003, despite an increase in workers' awareness of formal ethics programs. The survey also found reporting of misconduct was down by 10 percentage points. The survey of more than 3,000 American workers analyzes trends in workplace ethics, the implementation of formal programs, the ethical culture within organizations, the impact of programs, and factors that pose risks of misconduct. Some of its key findings include the following:

- 52% of employees observed at least one type of misconduct in the workplace in the past year, with 35% of those observing at least two or more violations.
- 69% of employees report their organizations implement ethics training, up 14 percentage points from the 2003 survey.
- 65% of employees indicated their organizations have a place they can seek ethics advice.
- 55% of employees who observed misconduct at work reported it to management, down 10 percentage points from the 2003 survey.

One critical finding of the 2005 survey is the importance of an ethical culture in organizations - the informal and social system that sets norms for the employee behavior and tells employees how things really work in that organization. The survey measures elements of an ethical culture such as the ethics-related actions of employees at all levels and perceptions of accountability for ethics violations.

All together now: "Armstrong will fire you for stealing. We'll do the same thing for lying."

Employees in organizations with a weak ethical culture reported a much higher level of observing at least one type of misconduct than employees in an organization with a strong ethical culture (70% compared to 34%). Those employees in organizations with a strong ethical culture like Armstrong International, Inc. were more likely to report the misconduct than those in weak-culture organizations (79% compared to 48%).

Culture had a stronger impact on the results of outcomes reported by employees than did formal ethics and compliance programs. In 2004, the U.S. Sentencing Commission recognized the importance of a strong ethical culture for organizational compliance.

"Creating a strong ethical environment should be a top priority of all companies," said Patricia Harned, President of the Ethics Resource Center. "We know formal programs are critical and work well initially, but we must now focus greater attention on building the right culture in which programs operate. This data shows, for example, that management needs to lead by example to set the tone throughout the whole organization." (1)

Good Corporate Citizens

Founded in 1987, *Business Ethics* magazine is the only U.S.-based business magazine focusing on ethics and corporate social responsibility. Published four times a year with a total distribution to approximately 10,000 readers, it has a unique position and a unique readership of thought leaders in business, investing, academia, government and civil society organizations interested in corporate social responsibility issues. Since 1999, the magazine has compiled an annual list of the "100 Best Corporate Citizens." The magazine considers factors such as environmental responsibility and fairness toward employees. They also rank companies on their accountability to the local communities in which they do business, ethics, and their ability to offer responsible products and services.

As you might expect the list is laced with big, popular companies with highly recognizable logos and names that have literally become household names. But then there are companies you have likely never encountered. For example, number one in 2007 for the second year in a row is tiny Green Mountain Coffee Roasters, Inc. of Waterbury, VT.

There are and always have been good and honorable companies, large and small, quietly doing what's right day in and day out, year after year.

With about 600 employees, Green Mountain generates revenue of more than $160 million. Each year the company's Director of Coffee Appreciation takes about a dozen or so employees on a trip to Vera Cruz and Oaxaca, Mexico. Here, employees visit coffee-growing cooperatives, pick coffee beans by hand and help sort them in the hot sun. They come away with a broadened view and a profound respect for the people who make up the human supply chain that brings coffee beans to their doorstep in Vermont. A genuine appreciation for the human side of their business is also evident in the $500,000 contribution Green Mountain makes each year to Coffee Kids. This is an international nonprofit group helping to improve the life and conditions of families working in the coffee industry. The company has contributed to the fund since 1988. (2)

Greed, theft and corruption still contaminate businesses worldwide. And most of the time that's what we hear about. We learn of the spectacular breaches in mortality because headlines scream at us about them. Most of the time, we conclude—and probably correctly so—that it's only the tip of the iceberg. The where-there's-smoke-there's-fire mentality sets in, and we come away from yet another business scandal unsurprised.

Companies like Green Mountain Coffee Roasters don't get many headlines, or at least the kind that make glitzy news. But their example is intoxicating proof that there are and have always been good and honorable companies, large and small, quietly doing what's right day after day, year after year. While it will never make the list of the year's 100 Best Corporate Citizens (because it is privately held), Armstrong International has been one of the good guys for 108 years. Let me show you a few of the reasons why.

Our Promise to Fred Kemp

*I*f an efficiency expert took a look at the layout of our screw machine and punch press division, he'd think we were crazy. The parts move from one end of our property to the other and back again in no logical order. All that travel means higher labor costs and lower productivity.

And I couldn't be prouder. Why? Well, the story really begins back in 1972. Back then it was clear that we'd need a new building to house our expanding screw machine and punch press departments. After much study and evaluation, we designed an addition that would keep the moving of unfinished goods to a minimum. The new building would be located right next to our old plant.

The layout was as efficient as could be. There was only one problem with the plan. It would require us to put the new building right where there was a home. The house belonged to Fred Kemp, then in his mid-seventies, who was a retired Armstrong employee.

The solution seemed simple. We'd buy Fred's house, tear it down and build the new plant next to the existing manufacturing plant. When we looked into the situation further, we found that we wouldn't even have to buy the house. We already owned it. The building committee went to the company President, Howard Lambertson, for permission to build.

The President vetoed the plan. "Fred has lived in the house forever," he said. "His children grew up there, and it really is the only place he's ever called home. I know he loves that place. We bought it from him years ago when it looked like we'd have to expand onto his property someday. But when we bought it, I promised he could stay there as long as he liked. We will keep our promise! We'll build the new plant on the other side of the property." This is one of the few times I am proud we are inefficient.

David's moral: *You can't put a price tag on integrity. You must always do the right thing no matter what it costs.*

I'll admit it: I get goose bumps every time I think about this one. No story makes me prouder to carry the Armstrong name. Talk is cheap, and it's easy to *talk* about doing the right thing and valuing employees (and former employees). But we *lived* the message when we made the decision to build the plant on the other side of the property. It sent a silent but simultaneously deafening message about trust and respect. One of the things about this story that makes me most proud is Fred's reaction. He learned early on that he could trust his company. So rather than hold out for an inflated price, he sold it to us at market value. In doing so, he fulfilled his part of the unwritten, unspoken covenant of trust and confidence that has existed between Armstrong and its employees from the very beginning.

You just can't fake ethics. Either you are or you aren't ethical. There is no middle ground. Ethics is a central part of the Armstrong pedigree. Clearly, we try to hire those who believe in our way of life. But sometimes a bad apple gets in, like the sales manager in this next story.

Points To Ponder From This Story:

1. **Live the message of your core values.**
2. **Show respect—to everyone.**
3. **You'll be repaid for doing what's right.**

Bribes

Let me share a story my father told me in a faraway place. The story starts with a phone conversation my father had with a salesman.

"Thanks for taking the time to talk with me today."

"It's my pleasure," said Gus.

"By the way, are you happy with the free gifts we sent?"

"What free gifts are you talking about?

The salesman continued, "Oh, you know, the wine, cigars, clothes, etc. we've been sending to your sales manager."

Confused, Gus answered, "I'm not aware of any free gifts."

The salesman explained, "Well, these gifts are sent often. It's common knowledge that your overseas sales manager expects to receive gifts in return for good service. Just ask any of the representatives."

Gus thanked the salesman for his time. "I will look into this matter. It is against company policy, and we will stop it immediately! I was not aware this was going on."

Gus Armstrong confirmed the facts by calling several overseas reps, all of whom gave the same story . . . the same sales manager had been receiving gifts for quite some time.

After summoning the sales manager to his office, Gus immediately questioned him. "I've just been informed you are receiving free wine, cigars and other gifts in return for service from our company. Are these stories true?"

"Yes, the stories are true, and I'll be happy to stop accepting free gifts immediately."

Gus responded quickly, "No, you don't understand! You knew this was against company policy. I'm afraid today will be your last day."

David's moral: *Knowing is not the same as believing.*

Hello?!? What part of "It's against company policy to accept bribes" didn't this guy understand? Come on, folks. You know when you're being bribed. Although it seems hard to believe, if you don't know, try a few simple tests. **Would you want your free gift reported in the company newspaper? Does this free gift benefit *only* you or does it benefit the whole company? Do you feel like you need to keep it a secret? Does it pass the smell test?** Remember, milk may look good, but a good whiff tells the real story. Your nose knows. Is a free sample a bribe? Depends. Was that free TV manufactured by the giver and was it intended for you or the company? If it was made by the giver, it's a sample. If the TV is for the company - you're probably okay. If not, can you say b-r-i-b-e? In some countries where wages are very low, bribes are a common practice to supplement income. The country's government probably knows about these bribes and allows them. Don't allow the "supplier" who lives in that country to take the lead. No one from your company should offer a bribe.

Remember those bad apples I mentioned? A few find their way into every company, I'm sure. The problem is that their dishonest tendencies drag down or dilute their real talents, so they are never able to realize their true potential. This sorry salesman is a case in point.

Points To Ponder From This Story:

1. **It's against Armstrong corporate policy to accept bribes.**

2.   **Apply the "bribe tests" if you're unsure.**
3.   **Foreign culture is not our culture.**

Liar, Liar Pants On Fire

*T*his is a salesman's sad story. It began with a trip to St. Louis, Missouri, followed by a trip to Stuart, Florida, for a meeting with Doug Bloss at Corporate. David Dykstra, Financial Controller for Armstrong-Hunt, Milton, Florida, reviewed the expense book of this salesman, and something didn't look right. Armstrong-Hunt is a small office, so David normally knew where everybody was going, and he didn't remember this trip being scheduled. He went to Larry O'Dell, General Manager of Armstrong-Hunt, to see if he could shed any light on the trip. Larry knew no reason for the salesman to meet with Doug. David Dykstra called Doug Bloss.

"Doug, I have an expense book that says one of our salesmen had a meeting with you last week. Is that true?"

"No, I didn't have any meetings last week."

"Do you know why this salesman would go to Stuart?"

"No, I don't have any idea, but you might want to check with Tom Clark. He might know."

David Dykstra called Tom Clark, the Sales Manager, who also informed David that he was unaware of any reason for the trip to Stuart and decided to confront the salesman when he visited the plant the following week.

Next week: "Good morning," Tom said. "I understand that you made a trip to St. Louis and then flew to Stuart to see Doug Bloss for a meeting."

"Yes, that's right. I had to make some coil calls, and then I flew down to meet with Doug."

"Well, how did you get home from Stuart when there's no airline ticket on our expense book?"

"Oh, I didn't take a flight home. I had to drive. You see, I bought a car when I was down there."

Tom sat silently in his chair. A few seconds passed. "You didn't go down to Stuart to meet with Doug Bloss."

"Yes, I did," the salesman insisted.

"No, you didn't! Doug told us he didn't have a meeting with you."

The salesman's face turned pale. His head dropped down, and he said softly, "You're right. I purchased a car near Stuart and I had to fly there to pick it up. I scheduled a flight from my customer to Stuart so I could drive the car back. I also charged a room and all my expenses during the day that I was on the road driving. I knew it was wrong. I was brought up better than that. I'll go along with whatever the company decides to do."

"The company has no choice," Tom said. "We'll have to fire you."

David's moral: *Honesty is always the best policy.*

This salesman knew the core values at Armstrong. He knew lying would get him fired. I know because I personally told him this several weeks earlier when I first met him. But he tried to beat the system and lost. Learn from his mistake and those of others around you. You won't live long enough to make them all yourself.

Points To Ponder From This Story:

1. **At Armstrong, lying will get you fired.**
2. **Learn from the mistakes of others; you can never live long enough to make them all yourself.**
3. **"Honesty is the first chapter in the book of wisdom." Thomas Jefferson.**

This next story is not about lying, but... well, I'll let you read it first.

R.H.I.P.

You have stumbled upon a tragic story which involves yours truly. Armstrong International had just introduced Armstrong Steam University on its Web page. The purpose of the online university is to impart knowledge on steam, condensate and air through a series of courses. If you feel brave, you can attempt to pass a series of tests. If you pass all six tests with 100%, you are rewarded with an Armstrong University T-shirt. On the T-shirt is our famous character and Web page course guide, Armey Steamstrong, who looks a little bit like Albert Einstein. These T-shirts are in high demand. Everybody wants one!

One day, I found myself at the doorstep of our Webmaster, Pam Blasius. "Hi, Pam. Could I have one of the Armstrong Steam University T-shirts?"

"Uh, sure, David. You know you're supposed to take the tests before I give you a shirt."

"Yeah, I know. I'm going to take the tests when I get home. I just thought I would get the shirt now."

"Uh, Okay. What size do you need?"

One week later, I received a letter in the mail from Dave Collins, an Armstrong Representative. The letter read: "The grapevine has it that the Chief Operating Officer has received an Armstrong Steam University T-shirt without passing the tests. While I was in the Army we had a saying, R.H.I.P.—*Rank Has Its Privileges*. David Armstrong is known for storytelling throughout the halls of Armstrong. Does he also want to be known for R.H.I.P?"

David's moral: *Power does not kill; it permits suicide.* —Earl Shorris, writer

Okay, okay. I knew better, but I took advantage of my authority and forced Pam to give me a T-shirt. That was wrong. I didn't lie for I took the test several times, but I never scored 100% because I didn't know how to look up steam charts to pass the test. Bravo David Collins for having the courage to set my moral compass back on target. I went astray. We as leaders are not perfect; we need brave souls to keep us from being corrupted by the power we possess. I apologized to Pam Blasius and to all the other people who have taken the tests and passed them. This story has been written to apologize to all who were cheated by my actions and to give Pam Blasius the authority to refuse to give an Armstrong Steam University T-shirt to anyone who has not taken and passed all the tests with a 100% score. And yes, I returned the T-shirt to Pam. My actions were wrong, but I confessed the error of my ways and made amends. Not so with the culprits in the following story.

Points To Ponder From This Story:

1. **I knew better. When your instincts speak, listen.**
2. **Leaders are not perfect.**

The Eighth Commandment

Thou shalt not steal. These words were spoken by God to Moses long, long ago. These words are good words to live by, especially if you are an employee of Armstrong International. If you break the eighth commandment, you should have concern about how you will be judged by God. And guess what? You'll have plenty of time to think about it, since you will be unemployed. Armstrong International will not tolerate stealing as some have found out the hard way.

There once was a salesman who sold materials to Armstrong International, Three Rivers, Michigan. One day he found himself tempted to break the eighth commandment. He noticed money lying out in the open in our cafeteria. Read my story, "Our Cafeteria," in *Managing By Storying Around* to understand why we have money out in the open. Nobody was watching—so he took it! On each visit, he would take money from the concession stand and then go to his first call in the plant. Within a short period of time, it became obvious that there was a thief among us. A trap was soon set. Before long, the salesman made another visit and stole some money from the concession stand. This time he was caught. Confronted, he denied that he was stealing, but we had the proof and sent him on his way, never to return.

There's another story told about a radio that turned up missing from the corporate office. Soon, several other items were found missing. Upon further investigation, it was revealed that all concession stand lunchrooms were having shortages in cash. We had a problem. We had a thief—a thief who was stealing on a larger scale, not just money. Again, we set a trap and very shortly caught the person. Again, this was not an Armstrong employee. He worked for the outside cleaning service. This person was confronted and never allowed to return to our company. There are possibly two more stories that I have not told, totaling four stories throughout the decades, where we had problems with people breaking the eighth commandment. Not a bad record, if you ask me. I wish the rest of society could brag as well.

David's moral: *Thou shalt not steal.*—Eighth Commandment, God

We've all heard the excuses: "I needed money;" "I didn't know any better;" "The company wasn't fair to me." There are probably as many excuses as the number of those caught stealing, but not one will save them. Never let your problems become an excuse to steal. You may be one of the company's best employees. You may be the most productive, brightest or most valuable. Yet with all these honors, if you steal, you are a thief. The result for a thief with honors is the same as for a thief with no honors. You will be fired.

It's this simple: Armstrong will not change its honor system. We will trust our people to come to work on time versus using time clocks. Our people pay their bills in the lunchroom on the honor system instead of to a cashier (wasted labor). Checking your own quality for mistakes is your responsibility, not that of the quality assurance department. We will continue that which has made us successful and unique from other companies—our honor system.

Points To Ponder From This Story:

1. **Don't let problems become an excuse for stealing.**
2. **Honor is better than honors.**
3. **Trust people, not locks.**

Let's Make a Promise To ...

"Promises we can begin keeping right here, right now." *David Armstrong*

- Put morality on the job 24 hours a day.
- Fire *any* employee who violates core values.
- Tell the truth so you don't have to remember what you said.
- Do unto others as you would have others do unto you.
- Don't just talk about the core value messages, *live* them.
- Remember that honor is better than honors.
- Learn from the mistakes of others; we can never live long enough to make them all ourselves.
- Accept the fact that people will always be tempted.
- Trust people, not locks.

Chapter Three

Blurring the Lines

The 1930's-style soda fountain, complete with vintage Coke dispenser and condiment wells, sits in the middle of the lobby of Biggs-Gilmore an advertising/marketing firm Armstrong has used since the 1970s in Kalamazoo, Michigan. I can remember many a meeting ending with all of us perched atop chrome-stemmed stools eating ice cream. It was the perfect blend of business and pleasure, and the soda fountain is a wonderful example of one of my most persistent obsessions—mixing fun with work. In fact, I don't want to settle for fun as something that happens after you leave work. I want it to be an important *part* of work.

I've never understood the idea that work is something to be endured in order to receive the rewards waiting at the end of the ordeal—a paycheck and the weekend. For the vast majority of workers in every field, work is serious business. And going to work is a lot like going to battle with crabby co-workers, ungrateful supervisors and rude, demanding customers. It is a joyless, thankless ordeal to be endured week after week, month after month, year after year. This is one's lot in life, many believe. It is how bread gets on the table, cars and trucks stay gassed up and on the road. It's the burden to be borne to keep a roof over the family's heads, clothes on their backs and, if you're especially lucky, an extra dollar or two in the bank.

People who look at work from this perspective draw thick black lines between the worlds of work and fun. Work is what you have to do to survive. Fun (personal home/family time, leisure)—and money, of course—are what you earn by working hard. The lines between these divergent worlds are hard, rigid and never to be confused. The boundaries, so the thinking goes, are just as sacred as the invisible lines on the ground separating one nation from another. Don't mess with them. Don't even *think* about messing with them. And whatever you do, never,

never let the boundaries become fuzzy or indefinite because elements of humor, laughter or enlightenment from the world of fun may leak into work.

I don't want to settle for fun as something that happens after you leave work. I want it to be an important part of work.

Let's hope so. I believe God intended us to enjoy work as much as the other parts of our lives. What's more, I believe those who have fun at work are more pleasant, happier, more productive and more open to new ideas and collaboration. If we really want employees to think like owners, let's create an environment where they can be themselves instead of robotic rule reciters. Let's trust them, laugh with them, support them in their failures and celebrate with them our collective successes. And let's have some fun while we're at it.

Mix It Up.

No, the sky won't fall. At least it hasn't in all the years I've been preaching and practicing the gospel of fun at Armstrong. Although some say I obliterate the lines between work and fun (and I have on occasion), I would settle for a permanent blurring of the lines. A little smudging, please. I would rather that employees never really know where the boundaries are. "When in doubt, have fun." That's my motto. I will always fight for a company that is fun for all, not just a privileged few. There are many ways to have fun—playing the game, which means being allowed to make decisions. Creating a small company gives you an environment where this can happen.

Or maybe it's having a facility like our recreation building with its big TV, pool tables, weight machines and a gymnasium for basketball and volleyball. Maybe it's waging a squirt gun war? Or perhaps it's posting colorful signs with funny messages. Maybe it's creating conference rooms that resemble castles or baseball stadiums. Maybe fun is putting an Oasis Park in the middle of the shop or letting employees, with great pride I might add, paint production machinery every color of the rainbow.

I don't want Armstrong employees to just exist. I want them to live—really live! I want them to be full of life and have a sense of adventure and discovery. I believe the imagination of our employees is one of our greatest assets. That imagination and creativity—and the freedom to express them—are big parts of our hope for the future. And we all lose if we don't create ways to set them free in a colorful, dynamic and unexpected workplace. Okay, I'll get down from my soapbox . . . for now. Let's get back to that soda fountain.

I believe those who have fun at work are more pleasant, happier, more productive and more open to new ideas and collaboration.

Emerson's Soda Fountain began life in Battle Creek, 20 miles or so east of Kalamazoo. When Bill Biggs, flamboyant founder of Biggs-Gilmore, caught wind of the fountain's planned demise, he snapped it up and had it installed in the lobby of the firm's offices at the corner of Portage and West Michigan. When the company changed owners and locations in the early 90s, the soda fountain went along. A decade later, three employees bought Biggs-Gilmore and moved the firm to a quaint, Chicago-style loft space a few blocks away. Once again, the new owners moved Emerson's pride—lock, stock and marble top. Today, it shares center stage with an antique jukebox in the sprawling lobby of the new Biggs-Gilmore. Nearby hangs a ceramic version of the Twister game and downstairs in a glass-fronted meeting room known to insiders as the Fishbowl, a foosball table waits expectantly.

First-time visitors pause at Emerson's, try out the stools and invariably ask, "Do you really have ice cream?" Always! Employees meet here for quick sessions with each other or suppliers. The soda fountain is the staging area for lunch dates, client outings and new business calls. The fountain is in attendance for every agency gathering, the host of every monthly birthday recognition and a part of every Christmas party. In short, employees have woven Emerson's into the fabric of Biggs-Gilmore, and I think the company and its people are better for it.

Fun... Not Just For Ad Agencies Anymore

But what do you expect? It's an ad agency, and those places are always a little weird, right? In fact, Bill Biggs used to give agency tours and with a wave of his hand characterize the Creative Department as ". . . the place where we keep the nuts." Well, I'm not an ad man. But if I ran an ad agency and my product was ideas, I think I'd want to do everything I could to create an environment that helped my people come up with ideas—lots of them. I'm guessing that the first step to spawning innovative, out-of-the-box thinking is getting employees into a work environment that mirrors what you want to achieve. That's probably why another ad agency, TBWA/Chiat Day in Los Angeles, has a full-size basketball court as a part of their office complex. But workspace inventiveness spreads well beyond the world of advertising. ABC News reported recently on Nike's headquarters complete with tennis courts, track fields and a swimming pool. And Google . . . well, hold onto your hats, ladies and gents, because what don't Googlers get? Their benefits include:

- On-site physician and dental at their Mountain View, California, and Seattle, Washington, locations
- Maternity and parental leave with an option to expense up to $500 in take-out meals during the first month following a baby's birth
- Bonus program for employee referrals
- Tuition reimbursement
- Adoption assistance
- Fuel Efficiency Vehicle Incentive Program
- Employee discounts
- On-site dry cleaning (1)

With nearly seven million subscribers browsing through some 80,000 titles, Netflix is the world's largest online movie rental operation. The company values employees who demonstrate judgment, productivity, creativity, intelligence, honesty, communication, selflessness, reliability and passion. And when it finds them, it rewards them with large salaries, virtually unlimited vacation time and generous investment vehicles. (2)

I'm guessing that the first step to spawning innovative, out-of-the-box thinking is getting employees into a work environment that mirrors what you want to achieve.

Clearly, Google and Netflix provide extraordinary benefits made possible by extraordinary success. While these perks are not precisely examples of mixing fun and work, their examples are instructive. Companies that can afford to give their employees virtually anything often choose to give them a freer, more creative work environment and experience. Such efforts go a long way toward making work more relaxing, less stressful and more fun. And I'm willing to bet that employees who enjoy their time on the job are likely to be more productive. According to a 2002 survey conducted by the Society of Human Resources Management 75% of the respondents believed that companies who had created a fun work environment were more effective that those who did not.

Help For The Hardnosed

At Play, a Richmond-based creative consultant, fun is a key ingredient in their work for clients from American Airlines and Coca Cola to Universal Studios and Walt Disney Parks & Resorts. Part of their approach is to pump up energy with ideas that delight, inspire and disrupt traditional thinking. And they practice what they preach. Brightly colored walls enliven their headquarters, they encourage restroom graffiti and, according to an article in the *Christian Science Monitor*, visitors shouldn't be surprised to see sidewalk musicians performing during the lunch hour.

Since 1975 Playfair has been helping companies have more fun at work. They even created an International Fun at Work Day in 1996. It's listed in Chase's Official Calendar of Events for April first (or the first Thursday in April if the first falls on a weekend). Their Web site (www.playfair.com) offers a list of fun ideas you can use or adapt to your needs. (My favorite is the Traveling Bouquet. It's an easy way to spread a little fun and get a lot of people involved. Just bring in a bouquet of flowers, present it to a coworker with instructions to pass it on after half an hour. Each person does the same.) The site also links to several others devoted to humor and fun in the workplace (www.deepfun.com, www.humorproject.com, www.cwmetcalf.com and www.allenklein.com).

Although some say I obliterate the lines between work and fun, I would settle for a permanent blurring of the lines. A little smudging, please.

Tory Johnson, founder and CEO of Women for Hire (www.womenforhire.com) and the workplace contributor for "Good Morning America," offers some helpful hints for adding fun to the workplace in simple, inexpensive ways. Her hints can limber up companies and employees and serve as good experiments to see how—and how far—fun and humor might travel in a work environment. For starters, you might have a ball. A mere $10 is all it takes (www.sendaball.com) to ship a brightly colored volleyball-sized ball to anyone you designate in the U.S. No elaborate packaging here. Your surprised recipient gets a ball stamped with a simple message: "Have a ball."

At www.mymms.com you can get the famous candies imprinted with a custom message or a company logo. If you have employees, coworkers or clients that take the cake, tell them so. Really. The folks at www.bakemeawish will send a variety of gourmet sweet treats on your behalf. At www.knockknock.biz you can get fun, clever office supplies to replace boring standard issues. At www.sillyputty.com, you can get enough of the stuff to bring a whole new kind of fun to an employee gathering, client meeting, sales conference—or just a tedious Thursday afternoon.

For those who are hesitant or afraid that introducing fun and humor into the workplace will somehow push them beyond the point of no return, reserve it for special occasions. Or use it as a carefully planned backdrop for incentives or rewards. Here's an example. When a dentist figured out he could afford to give each staffer a $200 bonus, he decided to have some fun with it. Rather than just rolling the extra cash into their checks where it would disappear in the name of some quickly forgotten obligation, he invested time and planning to make the reward truly meaningful and memorable. First he closed down the office for two hours and sent all the employees off to the local shopping mall where he gathered all of them around him in a circle.

Imagination and creativity—and the freedom to express them—are big parts of our hope for the future.

To each employee he handed an envelope with $200 in cash—and a set of rules: Whatever you buy is yours to keep. You must spend it only on yourself, and you have one hour to buy five different gifts. Any money not spent was to be returned. Then the good dentist sat back and watched the fun. At the next staff meeting, everyone brought in their treasures for a group show-and-tell. Don't have that kind of money to spend? No matter. It works just as well on a smaller scale.

When a director of a college food service heard about the dentist's fun reward, she adapted it to her budget and circumstances. She took her secretary out to lunch and had a heartfelt conversation expressing all the things she appreciated about her assistant but had never expressed. At the end of the lunch, she presented her with $50 and told her to take an hour off and go buy a nice present for herself. Adding fun to work is not risky, dangerous or foolhardy. In fact, it might just be the most enjoyable and least invasive way for you to knock down barriers, build up people, create lasting memories and maybe, just maybe, limber up rigid attitudes.

Some Work Too Serious?

Okay, I know you've been dying to say it, so go ahead.

Well, all that fun stuff is fine for some places, but a lot of work is just plain too serious. There are places where blurring the lines is not—will never be—appropriate or acceptable. Don't you agree?

I agree that every job has its serious side. You would be hard-pressed to find a company more committed to product quality and extraordinary customer service than Armstrong International. But I just don't think it's possible for me, or anyone, to sit in isolation and levy judgment across an entire spectrum of possibilities. I would rather reserve that judgment for employees in the thick of things—on the firing line, so to speak. If you have the courage to hire carefully, train appropriately and trust implicitly, I believe employees will rarely let you down. When they are encouraged to think like owners and know that they are trusted and empowered, they will virtually always make the right decision.

As far as some jobs just being too serious . . . I don't believe it. That is the convenient refuge of the narrow-minded and unbending. Sure, there are parts of every job where seriousness and attention to detail rule the day—and must. But to suggest that some businesses are just too serious to qualify for fun-on-the-job... Phooey, I say. Few businesses are as serious as running an airline. In this business, you launch your principal assets off into the wild blue yonder day after day, hurtling the most precious of cargoes—human lives—through the air at hundreds of miles an hour. What could be more serious?

That's your cue, Southwest Airlines. Front and center, please.

49

From its first flight in 1971, Southwest Airlines has been a poster child for coloring outside the lines. In fact, early recruiting ads actually used that image. (In 2006, the airline received an unbelievable 284,827 resumes for 3,363 positions.) (3) This is not a company that simply decided one day to be different by injecting fun into how they run their airline. Their absolute fanaticism about on-time service, cost containment and customer care are outgrowths of their difficult beginning and colorful past. Every employee of Southwest is devoted to what they regard as their crusade—bringing safe, convenient and affordable air travel to people who never thought they would be able to fly. They honestly believe they have made the world a better place—and continue to do so every day they uphold their outrageously high standards.

But to suggest that some businesses are just too serious to qualify for fun on the job... Phooey, I say.

Southwest has always done things other airlines believed were impossible or just plain crazy. Because they think like owners, believe in themselves (and know that the people at the top believe in them), they shrink from no challenge. Best of all, they are encouraged to have fun along the way. Management encourages them to be themselves and to act, think and perform independently but in line with clearly understood Southwest core values and principles of service. These are people who say, "I love you," on the job. They laugh, cry and hug each other. Southwest flight attendants have been known to pop out of overhead bins during preflight preparations. At Southwest, pilots help unload baggage and pick up trash after a flight. Like Armstrong International they have no job descriptions. At Armstrong we insist that everybody answer each others telephone within three rings. We don't provide job descriptions and inform our employees we don't because we want nobody to say, "That's not my job." We also remove any walls between departments so employees won't believe they only live to serve their department. All of this creates an environment where everybody does what needs to be done. At Southwest everyone does whatever needs to be done to keep flights flying on time, while offering topnotch customer service and low costs. Has it worked? You be the judge.

When Lamar Muse came aboard as Southwest's first CEO in 1979, the company had less than $200 in the bank and overdue bills totaling $80,000. (4) In

1989 Southwest's revenue surpassed the billion dollar mark, and year-end figures for 2006 confirm its 34th consecutive year of profitable operation. Today, Southwest's 33,000 employees make more than 3,300 flights flight each day. In 2006, the airline carried 96.3 million passengers.

Universally lauded, idolized, imitated and pedestalized, Southwest Airlines has won more awards than it can count and is a success by any standard you want to apply. Since the U. S. Department of Transportation (DOT) began tracking stats for customer satisfaction in the late 1980s, Southwest was the first airline to win first place ranking for Best On-time Record, Best Baggage Handling and Fewest Customer Complaints—the so-called Triple Crown. They did it first in May of 1988 and dozens of times since. They also racked up *annual* Triple Crowns in 1992, 1993, 1994, 1995 and 1996. Southwest has also pioneered many innovative programs. And they were the first with a frequent flyer program based on number of trips rather than the number of miles traveled.

Armstrong International is a specialist in steam, air and hot water systems. While our business may not be as exotic as running an airline, it provides plenty of opportunity for our people—and our customers—to mix fun with business. As long as I have anything to say about how our business is to be run, we'll continue to blur those pesky lines between work and fun.

A Case In Point

What does a game show have to do with the serious business of selling products to customers? Nothing . . . and everything. It depends on your point of view . . . and how broad your mind is. We had great fun with our customers by playing our own version of *Let's Make a Deal*. The customers loved it. They will remember it for a long time and, unless I miss my guess, will retell this story frequently . . . and with fond recollections of the company that brought it to them. They will remember that we didn't take ourselves too seriously to have fun. Did they have an enjoyable experience? Read this first story, and tell me what *you* think.

Let's Make an Armstrong Deal

"**W**elcome to **Let's Make an Armstrong Deal**", announces the game host. There, in front of the contestants, hang three curtains. The rules are simple: Choose one curtain and the prize behind it is yours. The prizes are Armstrong products ranging from several thousand dollars to a few dollars. The game host selects a customer wearing an Armstrong hat.

"Which curtain would you like?"

"I'll take, uh, curtain number two," answers the contestant.

"Before we show you what's behind curtain number two, let's see what's behind curtain number one." The curtain goes up and there sits a pumping trap valued at $2,000. The contestant sighs in disappointment.

"That's okay. There could still be a good prize behind curtain number two."

"I hope so. I am really hoping it's a water heater because we need one in our company."

"Well, how sure are you that it's behind your curtain? What if I were to give you a 5% discount?" The game host pulls out a wad of Armstrong discount dollar bills and places 5% in his hand. "Do you still want curtain number two?

"Yes."

"What if I gave you 10% or 15%?"

"Oh boy, 15% off my next purchase? No, I am going to stick with curtain number two."

"Well, let me show you what you would have won if you had chosen curtain number three." The curtain goes up and there behind it is an Armstrong-Lynnwood yellow steam hose. Value—$360. Everybody sighs.

"So, you're feeling pretty good about your choice?"

"Yes, sir. I just know it's a water heater."

"How sure are you? What if I gave you 20% off your next purchase?" The host places another 5% in the contestant's hand.

"I still want the curtain."

"Here's my final offer—25%."

In the audience you can hear his fellow classmates yell, "Take the discount! No, take the curtain!"

"What will it be?" asks the game host.

"The curtain. I'll take the curtain."

"Well, let's see what's behind curtain number two."

The curtain slowly lifts and there behind it is an Armstrong GP2000K1 pressure reducing valve. Value—$800. The contestant smiles with a sigh of relief and the audience cheers while the game host says, "Thank you for playing **Let's Make an Armstrong Deal**."

David's moral: *Both work and fun are more memorable when you blur the lines between them.*

The "contestant" was a customer attending Armstrong Steam University (ASU), and I was the game host. Our main purpose with the game was to have fun and to send one of our customers home with a prize, an Armstrong product. We knew when he took the product back to his company, he'd be a hero, of sorts. We also knew he would use the product and, hopefully, more of our products in the future. The way I look at it, even if we lost, we would still win. If the customer had picked the curtain hiding an expensive product, we win because he will be using our product in the end. Remember, these are mostly Armstrong customers coming to ASU. If they are not customers already, maybe having fun at Armstrong is all it'll take to convert them to buying our products.

How We Did It.

As for the discount, we decided to offer an extra discount on the next purchase of <u>one</u> item only. We printed up some Armstrong funny money in increments of 5%, which gave me a chance to lay 5% discount money in the hands of the customer. If they still chose the curtain, they had to return the discount paper money. If they kept the discount, the discount money was only valid if signed by a General Manager. And those curtains? They were actually overhead doors in the shipping department which we used to load trucks. We added painted numbers and painted curtains. This was the perfect location at the end of a tour, and we had plenty of space for thirty customers to sit back and watch one of their own play the "game." A couple of hints if you try this yourself: Pre-record some "audience sounds" (applause, sighs of disbelief and laughter) and play them at appropriate times. If this is too expensive or time-consuming, just make some cardboard signs and have some of your people hold them up as audience prompters. Also, sprinkle some of your people in the audience as plants to keep things lively.

I want a playground whenever I can get one—or make one. Sure, this could have been done much more quietly and simply. But where's the fun in that? Blurring the lines between work (business) and fun makes both of them more memorable. Actually, our game show was pretty tame, compared to what our people at Computrol do. See what I mean by reading the following story.

A Point To Ponder From This Story:

1. **Have fun. In this case, even if we "lost," we won. The customer will be using our product.**

Pie

The folks at Computrol in Boise, Idaho, know how to have fun at work. I mean they really know how to have fun. You may find this story hard to believe, but it is true. It begins with a blue tarp laid on the floor and up against the back wall in the lunch room. Then a large piece of plywood is placed in the center of the tarp. Three holes—large holes—are cut into the plywood. There is a line drawn across the floor twelve feet away. A table is set up next to the line. On the table are pie pans and cans of whipped cream. Written next to the holes in the plywood is the phrase, "For one buck, they can't duck." You guessed it. It's a pie-throwing contest, and for $1 anyone can throw a pie.

This story has a happy ending. Whom do you think the pies are thrown at? The management of Computrol, of course. Even the President. You should see the line of people, waiting to throw one—sometimes five—pies at their favorite (or shall I say unfavorite) leader. The leaders are good sports for allowing this to be done, and everyone has a good time. The money raised from this pie-throwing contest is used for their Christmas party at the end of the year. The folks at Computrol have several other unique ideas for raising money which I hope to share with you in the future.

David's moral: *Employees having fun is a necessity, not a luxury.*

Not only is laughter great medicine, it's a powerful weapon to use against complacency and taking yourself too seriously. It's not exactly a *secret* weapon, but you'd think so judging from how infrequently some companies use it. Laughter is Computrol's secret ingredient in the work/fun recipe. I say, let's share this secret with every Armstrong division. You can't appreciate how powerful laughter is until you hear it overcome people as they watch the pies start to fly. Picture this: A pie flops on top of a leader's head and whip cream drips down the sides of his face—all to the accompaniment of laughs, giggles and shouts of "Hooray!" I remember watching Tony Mariani take one to the face. What made it extra special was his heavy beard. Imagine the (funny) mess it made.

We simply spend too much of our life at work not to have fun while there. Work can be fun, no matter what anybody says. It just takes a little effort and some imagination. Computrol is proof of that. Why not try it at your company? And come on, Armstrongers, let's creatively swipe Computrol's pie-throwing idea and have some fun.

Laughter is no enemy to profits. People who laugh and have fun are better employees. They provide better service and will be more creative in developing new products and services. They will be quicker to please customers, be easier to work with, produce better quality and stay with your company longer. All of these things start with the willingness to laugh at and with each other. And they end in a more productive, pleasant and profitable company.

Points To Ponder From This Story:

1. **Laughter is Computrol's secret. Make it yours. Start today.**
2. **Make work fun. Improve service, quality, innovation, and reduce employee turnover.**
3. **Laughter is no enemy to profits. And ... it costs so little.**

Armstrong's Living Mural

Armstrong International, Michigan, offers technical product seminars. In these seminars, product specialists give presentations to our customers, sales force and new employees. Each of these product specialists provides technical training on Armstrong products. Today Chris Vogel, Product Specialist for

Armstrong pumping traps, is giving her presentation. At the closing remarks of her presentation, she wants to show how a pumping trap actually works.

"Would everybody please get up and follow me to Armstrong's living mural?" says Chris.

When each seminar guest exits the seminar room through the double doors, they immediately see a painted wall mural seven feet high and twenty-five feet long. It shows many Armstrong products. Painted on the wall is a portrait of the room they just left. Chris points down to a pumping trap, which is cut in half to show the working parts. The pumping trap is a real unit (not painted) that has been placed into the wall of the mural. There is glass piping going to it, which is also part of the mural. The pumping trap is actually working. Chris begins:

"In Armstrong's living mural, you will see our pumping trap. As the condensate from the equipment comes to it, the pumping trap fills up, thus raising the float. When the float rises, it allows the condensate to be discharged to an overhead return line back to the boiler."

David's moral: *Customers will remember what they learn if they're having fun learning it.*

Chris found a way to make learning about our products fun. She gave people a different way to think about our products and our entire company—and that positive predisposition toward Armstrong will probably make them more likely to buy Armstrong products. In short, she paid attention to the intangibles. Fun, pride and enthusiasm are things you can't quantify on a spreadsheet or chart. But they're the makings of enjoyable customer experiences, fulfilled and motivated employees and pleasant, positive memories for both.

Finding, supporting and keeping energetic employees who are willing to stretch their comfort zones is a big job, and it takes creative leaders to even *recognize* this potential when it surfaces at the interview stage. Employees like Chris prove daily that doing business with Armstrong isn't ordinary and humdrum. Customers like buying products from companies who have fun and who liven up the learning and buying processes. A decision to buy is not always based on price, quality, innovation or service. Of course, these things are essential factors, but customers like to buy from companies who make them feel good. So lighten up and have some fun... like the two characters in my story.

Points To Ponder From This Story:

1. Customers learn more if they're having fun.
2. Don't forget the intangibles.
3. Make the job fun for your employees. It doesn't have to cost much.
4. Pursue candidates who understand fun. Hire them, now!

Armstrong's Fire Department

*B*elieve it or not, Armstrong International has its own fire department. This department is large enough that we have our own fire chief and many volunteer firemen. One important thing was missing in this department besides the spotted dog. You guessed it—a fire truck. Armstrong-Yoshitake fixed that problem.

Armstrong-Yoshitake had purchased a used delivery truck. The motor was in good shape, but the body was falling apart with lots of rust and holes in the side panels. Don English and Mike Wolfe decided to pull off the panels and rebuild the truck. They ordered large sheets of stainless steel, which they bent into doors, panels and the cab. Once assembled, they painted it bright fire-engine red. Don had been given an aluminum ladder from the city's fire department because it was damaged. He cut a small piece from the ladder and attached it to the side of the new fire truck. An old piece of fire hose was neatly coiled in the truck. They even attached some red and white emergency lights to the cab. Don and Mike hope to find a siren which we've all heard as fire trucks race to a fire. Now the only thing missing is the spotted dog.

David's moral: *People succeed more often at their jobs when they have fun doing them.*

What does a smile cost anyway? However little it is, a smile provides an incredible return on your investment. A few chuckles will improve the morale of your people. Employees at Armstrong often do a better job if they have fun. They build better quality if work is fun. They work better together if having fun. Don and Mike use their fire truck to transport products the three blocks between Armstrong-Yoshitake and Armstrong International. The fire truck is faster than using forklifts, so it's more efficient. Besides, when's the last time a forklift provoked a smile or laugh? Speaking of smiles and laughs, they're an important part of Willie Vedmore's role at Armstrong, as this story will demonstrate.

Points To Ponder From This Story:

1. **Everybody talks about physical fitness but don't forget about mental fitness—the morale of your people.**
2. **People rarely succeed at anything unless they have fun doing it.**

Court Jester

This mysterious object was difficult to identify. There it was and there was no denying it. Its bright colors of red, purple, yellow and orange brought it to life. The three little balls seemed to dance in the air. There was shape to it, yet it had no shape. It seemed to go in all directions like it had a mind of its own. It was the perfect hat for Armstrong's Court Jester, Willie Vedmore. You've seen these hats in books or maybe in a circus or at the Las Vegas Cirque du Soleil show. Actually, that's where I purchased the hat, knowing it was the perfect costume for Willie Vedmore, who had just been promoted to Armstrong Court Jester. I presented the hat to Willie in front of his apprentice James Bucholtz, who was more than 20 years younger and looked forward to the day when he could become Court Jester.

I gave the Court Jester hat to Willie and said, "You know, Willie, this is part of your costume as Armstrong's Court Jester. You've got the business card that says Court Jester and now you have the hat."

"Thanks, David. I really like it!" Willie placed it on his head.

"No, Willie, you've got it on backwards. I want to make sure that you put it on right because you have to wear it around the company."

"This is perfect timing. I have a meeting in fifteen minutes. I'll wear it there."

"I was hoping you would say something like that, Willie. If not, I was going to take away your title and give it to James. You have to be willing to dress and act the part if you want the title of Court Jester."

Later that day I found Willie in his office. "How'd it go, Willie, with the hat at that meeting?"

"David, they loved it. It was a pretty serious meeting about production control, but when I wore the hat, it broke the tension in the meeting. I told a couple of jokes, and after that things went pretty smoothly."

"Outstanding, Willie. I knew I didn't make a mistake when I promoted you to Court Jester."

David's moral: *Make fun a priority in your business even if it stretches comfort zones.*

A few years earlier, in front of 300 people, I made an announcement that Willard Vedmore, who was a Production Manager, would be given a second title—*Court Jester*. It was difficult standing in front of my peers and promoting something they might consider foolish. But then I remembered the first time I asked Jan Blasius to dress up as a ballpark vendor for Armstrong Stadium. Asking her to wear a red and white striped outfit and sunglasses while carrying a tray filled with bags of popcorn and soda was not easy. But Jan did it and had a good time. Remembering Jan's laugh as she wore her vendor's costume gave me strength. Make fun a priority in your company even if, in the beginning, it makes you uncomfortable.

Points To Ponder From This Story:

1. Many things are difficult before they are easy.
2. All things are easier when done willingly.

Let's Make a Promise To …

"Promises we can begin keeping right here, right now." *David Armstrong*

- Blur the lines between fun and work.
- Create a playground.
- When in doubt, have fun.
- Don't settle for fun as something that happens *after* work. Make it a *part* of work.
- Harness the power of laughter.
- Let customers have fun. They will remember more if they have fun while learning.
- Attend to the intangibles. Fun, pride, and enthusiasm are things that can't be found on a spreadsheet, yet they make or break a company.
- Put fun into work and increase the likelihood of success on the job.
- Make fun a priority in business even if it stretches comfort zones.

Chapter Four

Giants at Work

Every time I see those temporary "Men at Work" signs along the road or the little tent placards at a store's entrance warning me of a slippery floor, I think of the signs I should make. They would use the same eye-catching black and yellow color scheme, but they would read simply, "Giants at Work." And I'd put them at every entrance of every Armstrong location around the world. Because we do employ giants, and every day they come to work and do their large and miraculous things and think nothing of it. Unfortunately, those of us in management sometimes think nothing of it, too—or at least too little of it. That's the job of the signs, to remind me and others of the giants among us.

If you were to stand by the door, you couldn't really tell which ones were the giants—unless you were a regular at Armstrong. You wouldn't see them duck to get through the doorway. Most of them don't stand any taller than the rest of us. They don't have huge feet or giant hands. And they don't talk with booming voices. In fact, just the opposite is true. Some of them are of slight stature, shy and retiring by nature and speak with hushed tones. It is, of course, their *contributions* which loom large, dwarfing everything around them.

The most incredible thing about all of this is that virtually every Armstrong employee is capable of being a giant on any given day. It all depends on what the day dishes out to them and to what opportunities they'll have to respond. Some are giants on a regular basis. Others rise to the occasion like an athlete coming off the bench to have a career-high game because something very important is on the line. What's on the line every day at Armstrong International is customer satisfaction. With each dawn comes a new challenge to deliver quality products wrapped and protected in a memorable, enjoyable experience.

Every Armstrong employee is capable of being a giant on any given day.

How do they do it? They employ my seven Ss. They think like entrepreneurial owners. They take responsibility. They apply the Golden Rule. They make decisions. Above all, they just plain manage. They manage to get over, under, around or through whatever obstacle confronts them. They get it—without being told or reminded or having a picture drawn, a hint dropped, a call made, a glance exchanged or a note written. They get what it means to be a trusted employee because they see Armstrong trusting them. If employees are to trust the company, the company *first* needs to trust the employees. That's why I am so immensely proud that we have giants at work. And it's why someday I'll make those signs.

Trust Lubricates Our Operation

In many companies rigmarole robs talented giants of their fearless instinct and talent, bogging them down and standing in their way. Talent plus trust is the combination that makes Armstrong's systems work. Trust is what frees talent to flourish. Here, employees freely apply judgment, timing and initiative based on the needs of the situation. It's what we expect of them, and it's also what they've come to understand as their responsibility. We're big on self at Armstrong. As in self-inspection. Self management. Self control. There is an unwritten agreement about the roles of employers and employees. It's a relationship built on the confidence that has existed for every year of our 108-year history. Sons and daughters of parents who worked at Armstrong grew up with Armstrong culture being discussed at the dinner table. They get it because they grew up with it. Their family code of behavior was mixed with their parents' ethics from work. These sons and daughters won't let Armstrong down. And people wonder why I get excited about hiring employees' children. My brother Patrick and I grew up with the company culture at home, and we too won't let these sons and daughters down.

Armstrong has never laid off a single full-time employee at our Three Rivers plants in 108 years. We have furloughed temporary workers on occasion. And there was a need to close a satellite foundry that had outgrown its usefulness. We have even closed a plant in Florida, a start-up in South Carolina and Germany when there was no hope of success. These decisions were most difficult, and it usually took years and large losses before we closed the doors. But we've never laid off a worker at our original plant site or our Belgium and China operations. Yes, we've fired people for violating clearly communicated core values. If we weren't willing to do so, they wouldn't be very core, would they?

How have we managed no layoffs for more than a century? Sometimes, it has been by putting our people to work on community projects in Three Rivers, Michigan. At other times, it was by reconfiguring shifts so that everyone worked less, but everyone worked. This happened during the Depression of the 1930s. On other occasions, it was by focusing people on internal projects. While such decisions may have nicked our profits slightly (and temporarily), it was a better course than cutting into company morale. Full, steady employment is something the Armstrong family and our extended family of employees have worked hard to achieve. And we're proud of it. We do what others cannot do. And for a variety of reasons, we have been fortunate—more fortunate than many employers and employees at other times, in other places and in other circumstances.

Trust Is What Frees Talent To Flourish.

Downsizing, right sizing, managed staff reductions, layoffs. If you're on the receiving end, it doesn't really matter what it's called. The result is the end of something definite and the beginning of something very indefinite, undefined and just plain scary. According to www.familyeducation.com, downsizing claimed some 10 million jobs in the last two decades of the last century. And it's not like the turning over of a century drew a magic line in the sand marking the end of this practice. Job losses in many industries have continued well beyond 2000. The U.S. auto industry continues to struggle with both Ford and General Motors recently announcing massive cuts. GM, for example, announced it was cutting 30,000 positions in 2005.

In the pharmaceutical industry, Merck cut 7,000 positions. A feeding frenzy among many other companies resulted in a nearly 90% increase in the number of jobs lost due to mergers and acquisitions in the same year. What's more, JP Morgan shared plans to hire 4,500 graduates in India over a two-year period. Cisco Systems announced plans to multiply its number of workers from India over two years. Other tech companies, including Microsoft, are following suit. All of this in 2005, per Challenger, Gray and Christmas, the outplacement firm. A news release of the U.S. Bureau of Labor Statistics noted that the trend continued right up through the spring of 2007. In March, for example, the BLS reported 1,276 companies laid off at least 50 people. The total number of workers involved was 130,687.

A number of factors account for job losses, including outsourcing. Ironically, Armstrong International was ahead of its time in introducing Armstrong Service, Inc. —a subsidiary of Armstrong International, Inc.—in the 1990s. Although Armstrong Service Inc. may have accounted for a small number of jobs being lost in client companies, that was never the intention. In fact, some of our strategies actually led to Armstrong hiring these very same customers' employees and always with the blessing of the employee and customer.

Armstrong Service, Inc. is our recognition that competitive pressures may have squeezed out of many businesses the very assets owners need to optimize utility systems. In-house utility expertise. People. Financing muscle. Without them, owners just can't reach the goal of optimized utilities. In many cases it is clearly Armstrong to the rescue because our brand can be summarized with 4E's— Energy efficiency, Environment, Enjoyable experiences and Education.

They get what it means to be a trusted employee because they see Armstrong trusting them.

Success in today's brutally competitive business environment depends on an ability to re-tool energy management tactics to keep pace. It requires more than out-of-the-box thinking. Sometimes it means flattening the box and making something new. And now, more than ever, it means finding partners who will provide far more than products. That's where Armstrong Service, Inc. comes into the picture. We provide the talent needed to recognize utility system inefficiencies, the manpower to implement the project ideas and the financing to fund the work necessary to optimize the plant. As a global leader in utility system optimization, Armstrong recognizes that every business has distinctly different operations, priorities, budgets and core competencies. That's why we emphasize flexibility as a key ingredient in our individual solutions—based on site-specific details.

Shouldering Responsibility

For many workers, a job is validation of their worth and meaning. It is a sense of identity and purpose. Moving from employment to joblessness is a tough passage, and it can be a cruel turn of life's path that requires years of recovery. Burning bridges and getting even are obvious temptations. But they are never productive or useful outlets. Job loss may be especially tough on sole bread winners, and the event can trigger isolation, fear, anger and feelings of worthlessness and deep depression.

Sometimes, of course, life has something better in store. Many look back on a job loss as the switch that turned their life into something bigger and better than it ever would have been under the previous circumstances. In the early 90s, Craig Newmark was 50ish and out of a job, having been downsized out of his spot as an IBM systems engineer. He moved to San Francisco to start over. In 1995 he started an e-mail list mailing alerts to his friends about "arts goings-on" in the San Francisco area. It grew and in six months he had almost 250 names. He turned it into a simple Web site because the volume was giving his e-mail fits. Before long, people were sending in messages about anything and everything—finding a roommate, getting a job, selling household items. The remarkable classified advertising site Craigslist was born, and two years later it was logging a million page views a month. Today, Craigslist has a staff of eighteen and revenues estimated at $10 million. Craig, by the way, still resists multimillion dollar buyout offers and tools around San Fran in his Toyota Prius hybrid. (1)

At Armstrong, employees freely apply judgment, timing and initiative based on the needs of the situation. . . . It's what they've come to understand as their responsibility.

A California home improvement center fired friends Arthur Blank and Bernie Marcus in 1978 after a union dispute. Deciding that they'd had enough of working for others, they set about turning hardware retailing on its ear. Their big box concept for hardware became Home Depot, and their first store opened in Atlanta later the same year. On opening day, the newspaper failed to run the Home Depot ad. No matter. Grand Opening sales generated so much money that their bank started asked questions about how a brand new business could have so much cash.

Home Depot sales topped $1 billion for the first time in 1986. The once jobless friends Blank and Marcus are now billionaires and then some, and Arthur Blank recently spent more than half a billion to acquire the Atlanta Falcons. (2)

While these stories are fun and the stuff of late-night fantasies, they are one in a gazillion. And for every one of these Grand Slams, there are countless strikeouts and downward spirals ending in depression, violent crime, divorce or suicide. I can't pretend to know what it feels like to lose your job. I've never been in that position. But I can guess that there is an enormous sense of betrayal. Fortunately or unfortunately, a good many workers in America have grown up in secure industries safe from layoffs and shielded by unions which have won for them high wages, incredibly generous vacation, health insurance and various other benefits they have come to expect as their due. Somewhere along the line, they have abdicated their responsibility for taking care of themselves and have forced it on to their employers or the government or sometimes both.

Faced with a job loss after many years of coddling and protection, some workers are simply unwilling to once again shoulder the responsibility for taking care of themselves. Stubborn and embittered, they squander time feeling sorry for themselves, bemoaning their misfortune and vainly searching for someone or something to come along and bail them out. When a major refrigerator plant closed in a small mid-Michigan town after providing decades of solid employment, workers were lost. It was the end of the world as they knew it. Now don't misread me here. This was a tragic situation, impacting nearly 3,000 lives and livelihoods. But I simply can't understand how grown men and women in such situations can resign themselves to self-pity and a persecution complex lasting at least as long as their unemployment checks.

I can understand why they don't want to start over. I can grasp the resistance to the intimidating task of retraining and trying to master and apply new, unfamiliar skills. But nothing can equip me to understand why adults who have little, do nothing to change their lot in life and then still complain that they have little. I think I can understand what it means to be a victim. But I can't comprehend why someone chooses to remain a victim through deliberate indifference and inaction. Yes, bad things *do* happen to good people, but I believe good people who have the desire for the world to be different can turn the tide in their favor. Unfortunately, I think the denial of personal accountability goes far beyond the unfortunates who are victims of job loss. I think there are vast numbers of people out there who simply believe that the world owes them pretty much anything they want.

Dealing With Results

"Rejection is what others do to you," a wise mentor told me once, "but failure is what you do to yourself." Basking in the light of a good result doesn't necessarily mean you're a raging success. And staring into the teeth of a bad result certainly doesn't mean that you are a dismal failure. Life is full of results—good, bad and every gradation in between. A result is just that. It is the attitudes, reactions and emotions through which we filter them that flavors these results as good or bad. Getting a bad result, even a string of bad results one after another doesn't mean that you've failed and will never recover. It just means that you need to carefully look at what preceded the result(s) so you'll know what to avoid the next time. Although I've interpreted this idea and put it in my own words, it is the essence of what Stephen Covey talks about in his *Seven Habits of Highly Effective People*.

In his book, Covey talks about the space that exists between stimulus and response. This space gives us the opportunity and ability to choose what our response will be. If you have a run-in with a coworker at 8 a.m., you can be upset and angry all day . . . or not. It is your choice. To illustrate his point, Covey invites his readers to carefully consider the very word *responsibility*. When you do, you will see that it is "response-ability." Or, literally, the ability to choose how you will respond. (3) I have a quote in my golf locker that I refer to often.

Attitude

"The longer I live, the more I realize the impact of attitude on life. Attitude, to me, is more important than facts. It is more important than the past, than education, than money, than circumstances, than failures, than successes, than what other people think or say or do. It is more important than appearance, giftedness or skill. It will make or break a company... a church... a home. The remarkable thing is we have a choice every day regarding the attitude we will embrace for that day. We cannot change our past . . . we cannot change the fact that people will act in a certain way. We cannot change the inevitable. The only thing we can do is play on the one string we have, and that is our attitude. I am convinced that life is 10% what happens to me and

90% how I react to it. And so it is with you . . . we are in charge of our attitudes. Charles Swindoll.

As I said earlier, I think the failure to shoulder personal responsibility goes well beyond those who are unwilling to be proactive after a job loss. Disagree? Let's examine some evidence. Nowadays, a lot of people find it easier to sue someone for their bad choices rather than accept the responsibility themselves. And even though we are sometimes amused by ludicrous nature of these cases, shouldn't we be outraged? Someone eats fast food several times a week and gets fat. (Now, there's a shocker!) Maybe they should just say to themselves, "Boy, that wasn't too smart. I need to change my eating habits." But no, they sue the fast food joint. Not your fault that you smoked for 30 years and now have cancer? Really? And whose fault is it? Oh, the tobacco company. I see. Well, better sue them.

On his Web site, www.overlawyered.com, Walter Olson chronicles frivolous lawsuits from around the world. There you can read about a case in which a 15-year-old female McDonald's worker had a year-long affair with her 22-year-old manager. Now that they have broken up, she is suing the restaurant for letting it happen. A New Hampshire man ticketed for speeding four times recently is suing the state's Department of Transportation. The suit demands a complete review of traffic and speed limits to see if they should be raised. In Sweden, a court ruled that the prison system could not restrict a convicted rapist's access to porn while behind bars. A Michigan woman is suing Mars, Inc. for $25,000 because its Starburst product is "dangerously chewy." And so it goes. See any personal responsibility here? Many blame the lawyers, but it takes you and me to hire these lawyers. The outrageous claims paid by courts are the fault of the jury members. Again, that's you and me. It is not the system. A system takes no action. It is the people who use it.

Giant Contributions Or Pygmy Attitudes?

But it gets better—or worse, depending on your point of view. In a January, 2007, address entitled "The Importance of Disease Prevention and Personal Responsibility" acting U.S. Surgeon General Kenneth Mortisugu lists five key factors in preventing most chronic diseases: tobacco control, good nutrition, physical activity, maintaining healthy weight and regular health screenings. Clearly, all of them are rooted in personal responsibility. But there's the rub.

According to the good doctor, America is largely health illiterate, and there are 90 million of us who simply don't know how to take care of our own health or prevent disease. You didn't buy that, did you? Neither did I. Heck, my kids learned all of this in grade school. We know what we must do, but we don't do it. "I do not exercise. I eat poorly—love the sugar and fat. But that's okay because I don't drink or smoke." Sound familiar? Don't fool yourself, we will find a way to justify what we do. I take full responsibility as should you. Keep it out of the courts and don't blame God when bad things happen to you because of your bad choices.

Dr. Mortisugu goes on to share some eye-opening facts about smoking. Even though it is the single largest preventable cause of disease, disability and death in the United States, there are still more than 44 million of us who choose to smoke. Each year about 440,000 will die prematurely of a tobacco-related disease. Today, the use of tobacco is the leading preventable cause of death in the U.S. Apparently, some people will die before they accept responsibility for their own actions.

I am convinced that life is 10% what happens to me and 90% how I react to it.

If those refusing to take responsibility for their own actions don't die of tobacco use, they might just starve to death. According to an April 11, 2007, press release by the highly respected Employee Benefit Research Institute (EBRI) reporting the results of the 2007 Retirement Confidence Survey, "Almost half of workers saving for retirement report total savings and investments (not including the value of their primary residence or any defined benefit plans) of less than $25,000. The majority of workers who have not put money aside for retirement have little in savings at all: 7 in 10 of these workers say their assets total less than $10,000." (4)

The likelihood of having inadequate funds for general living expenses is scary enough. But on top of that, many workers preparing for retirement are woefully ill-prepared for the cost of health care they will need in later years. "One recent EBRI study calculated that, assuming Medicare benefits remain at current levels, couples will need approximately $300,000 to cover health expense in retirement if living to average life expectancy, and as much as $550,000 if living to age 95." (5)

"In addition, more Americans are working into older age. As the baby-boom generation ages, the U. S. labor-force participation rate is increasing for those age 55 and older. The increase for those ages 55-64 is driven almost exclusively by an increase of women in the work force. However, the labor force participation rate increased for both men and women age 65 and above. . . . The reason: Workers face more responsibility in paying for their retirement expenses, as they depend primarily on a 401(k)-type plan (financed at least partially with their own contributions) and are increasingly expected to cover their own costs of health insurance in retirement." (6)

Yes, I still believe in the giants at work in your company and ours. But I believe they work side by side with pygmies—other workers whose lack of personal responsibility, bad attitudes and the-world-owes-me-a-living postures threaten to rot companies from the inside out. Giants will always survive, but it makes me angry to reflect on how their contributions are eroded or negated by the pygmies chirping around their ankles. In this case, might really does make right. So meet a few of Armstrong's giants.

The Chauffer

"Come, James." The company car slowly pulls out of the parking lot of Kangsen-Armstrong. Kerry Phillips sits quietly in the backseat looking out the window at the sights of China. He had been living in China for almost two years and still enjoyed looking at the sights. The silence was broken as James spoke.

"Zhou guai."

"Yes, left turn," Kerry repeats. The car stops in front of the Swissotel. Kerry says, "Ming tian jin?"

"See you tomorrow," repeats James.

The next day...

After another fun day of work, Kerry was ready to go home to his hotel in Beijing. As he came out of the doors of Kangsen Armstrong, he approached James at the company car. "I'm ready to go home."

"Just a few more minutes. I am not done cleaning the car."

Kerry quietly waited as James continued to clean the car. This was not the first time. Within a few minutes, Kerry was on this way home, once again gazing out the window looking for new sights.

David's moral: *Encourage your employees to think like entrepreneurs.*

We want our employees to think like entrepreneurs so Kerry was delighted that James treated the company car as a possession of the James Yang Limousine Company. If employees believe they are independent businesses, they will manage themselves. Rather than be mad that James wasn't ready to leave, Kerry was proud of him. He would never complain because he wants to keep the spirit of intrapreneurship alive in James. Remember, small self-directed companies are more focused on what they do, are streamlined and take risks. Do you think James would have cared about the dirt if he had viewed the car as a company asset rather than his personal possession and responsibility?

Points To Ponder From This Story:

1. **Ask your people to think and act like owners.**
2. **Keep it small. Large divisions can spin off small companies.**

The Cafeteria

At 11:55 a.m. every workday a whistle blows. It's lunchtime. And as you enter the Armstrong cafeteria, nothing—at first—appears out of the ordinary. There are picnic tables, refrigerators filled with sandwiches and soft drinks for sale, coffee machines, microwaves, candy machines . . . but wait a minute. The vending machines are unlocked, and there is no cash register. There is no one watching either the food or the money.

The cafeteria is run completely on the honor system. Employees pay for their food by putting their money into an open coin box. On a typical day the box will be filled with well over $100. This system works just fine.

David's moral: *If you believe in your employees, reward them with trust. If you don't, get rid of them.*

I believe self-control is the best control—whether you're talking about quality control, work attendance or paying for food in the cafeteria. Armstrong doesn't have time clocks, yet few people are late for work. Armstrong believes in self-inspection, and the proof that it works is our scrap rate at 0.4 percent. At Armstrong, people don't steal from the concession stand, even though there is unattended cash out in the open. Armstrong people have made me right time and time again: Give people responsibility for their actions, and they'll virtually always do the right thing. By getting rid of locked boxes and needless supervision, you're telling people you believe in them. Our employees have rewarded us a thousand fold in higher productivity and new ideas.

Get rid of locks, and you do away with secrecy. Contrary to popular opinion, sharing information gives you more control than withholding it. Think about it: In the absence of Big Brother, people are eager to impose controls on themselves. They *want* the responsibility for doing so. In one Armstrong division, we found employees consistently came in under budget when we put them in charge of the department's finances. Once they knew they had the final authority for spending, they didn't buy anything they didn't absolutely need. But go slowly. Introduce self-control to your company slowly. Make a change every few weeks. Observing how their leaders are treating them, your people will eventually believe they have control and reward you for it, just as our new employees at Everlasting Valve did.

Points To Ponder From This Story:

1. **Self-control is the best control.**
2. **Be open.**
3. **Don't expect quick results.**

The Time Clock

*A*rmstrong International had just acquired Everlasting Valve, a union shop with a traditional type of labor-management relationship, and our managers wanted to show the employees how *we* did things. Without consulting anyone at Corporate, the managers decided to remove the time clock. "If we really believe our people are our strongest asset, then we should treat them as if they are," the managers said to themselves. "Why should we have a time clock that humiliates them? They're adults. They know what time they are supposed to be at work. They know what's expected of them."

The managers went into the shop and took down the clock. Talk has always been cheap, but here was a group of leaders who, through their actions, were making it clear to their people that they believed the people they worked with were important and trustworthy.

How did the union employees react? They were shocked. At first, they expected the time clock would be used as a negotiating tool during the upcoming contract talks. But the fact that the management wanted nothing in return proved to them that they really were trusted.

The employees have proved they're worthy of that trust. We haven't had a problem with people coming in late. In fact, some people are now coming in early.

David's moral: *People know what time it is. If they don't, a time clock won't get them to work on time.*

Do what's right because it's right, not because you can use it as a bargaining chip. It's a question of respect. Respect your people, and they will reward you. What's more, letting people on the front lines handle such issues as the time clock has a dual benefit. It wins their respect because you trust them with making the plant productive. And it gives them a tangible symbol (removing the clock) to win the respect of their people. Win/win/win. "Do it because I say so," works with children (sometimes). But for adults, respect will carry the day every time. And speaking of respect, yours truly had to earn it the hard way, as the next story will prove.

Points To Ponder From This Story:

1. **Do the right thing—willingly.**
2. **Delegate to those on the front lines.**
3. **Listen to your people.**
4. **Treat employees with respect.**

The President's Son is Late for Work

$\mathcal{I}$t is a day in 1977 and as I'm driving to work, I realize I'm going to be late. As I get out of the car, I think to myself, "Oh boy, I'm late. I wonder if I can sneak in. I'm only a few minutes late—maybe no one will notice me."

So I pick a side door and quickly try to slip in. When I take a few steps, I hear that familiar sound... **Bam, Bam, Bam**. As it echoes through the factory from all four corners, the noise gets louder and louder . . . **Bam, Bam, Bam**. I thought, "I know what that sound is. It's the sound of hammers hitting the benches of all my friends in the factory." This is the tradition at Armstrong International, Inc., Michigan, when someone comes in late—they hammer you in.

Well, let me tell you, I was embarrassed! I immediately put my head down and went to my bench. Later that day, everybody was joking and teasing me and asking how I felt. I don't think I was late the rest of the summer, but I did have the opportunity to hammer in others who were late.

The year is now 1991, and I am visiting the Milton, Florida, plant. Employees have just finished watching a videotape about Armstrong where they saw the people in the factory hammering someone in as a demonstration of how to help support self-management. As I talked to several guys in the plant at Milton, they told me, "David, we just saw the video. We want you to know we started hammering people in when they are late. It really gets their attention!"

As I approached the next guy, I asked, "What do you think about hammering in people who are late?"

"Let me tell you, David, they hammered me in not once, but twice. I didn't like it. It's embarrassing. It makes you not want to come in late again."

"I know that feeling. It happened to me."

"You mean they actually hammered you in?"

"Everybody gets hammered in," I replied. "There are no exceptions."

David's moral: *You can hide from your boss but not from your co-workers.*

I believe in self-management. But I also believe it occasionally needs a boost from co-workers. There are times when fellow workers can help enforce self-management—like the time they hammered me in. The experience taught me a profound lesson: You can hide from your boss, but not from your co-workers. Of course, there are those rare situations when an employee can't manage himself and co-workers can't help. Then management needs to step in to enforce the rules.

At Armstrong, anyone can be hammered in. There are no exceptions—not even the son of the President. Or maybe *especially* the son of the President. At any rate, the sound of scores of hammers hitting workbenches is a sound I will never forget. It embarrassed me. It made me uncomfortable. And it made me a better person. The experience is not worth the extra few winks you'll enjoy by being late. Take it from David Armstrong, a guy who learned it the hard way.

Points to Ponder From This Story:

1. **Self-management needs support from co-workers.**
2. **Anyone can be hammered in. There are no exceptions.**

A Bad Four-Letter Word

This story begins in our room called "Seeing is Believing." In this room we show customers how our products work—under glass. The customers don't have to take our word for it. They can see it beneath the glass, hence the name—"Seeing is Believing." During one of the seminars a customer approached David Casterline during a break.

"Excuse me, David. You took us on a plant tour and showed us how you make your products. You also told us the culture of Armstrong is to trust employees. I saw this trust being practiced throughout the company, but I have a question." The customer pointed to a storage cabinet next to the steam trap board but said nothing.

"What's your question?" asked David as he looked at the storage cabinet.

"Isn't that a bad four-letter word?" He pointed again to the storage cabinet.

"What's a bad four-letter word?" repeated David.

"The l-o-c-k, David. The lock you're using to lock up the storage cabinet. I didn't see any locks in the shop, and you were bragging about it. But here we find one. Why?"

"That's a good question. I don't even know what's in the storage cabinet. We missed that one. We'll take care of it right away. Thank you for bringing it to our attention." David went into the lab and had one of the lab technicians bring out a hacksaw. They cut the lock off in front of the customer.

"There. How's that?" asked David.

"Wow! You really do trust your employees. I didn't think you'd cut it off now."

"This is serious stuff."

David's moral: *Armstrong International takes pleasure in doing what people say cannot be done.*

Okay, so we goofed. We forgot a lock. But we're light years ahead of most companies in this regard who never take the first step. Think of the courage it took the first time for Armstrong put its money where its mouth was about trust. We're not disappointed that a customer found a lock. After all, "You may have to fight a battle more than once to win it." So said Margaret Thatcher, former Prime Minister of England. The battle in this case is for the *belief* in trusting our employees without locks.

David Casterline brags about the Armstrong culture to each and every customer seminar group—and well he should. He has a right to brag. We all do. Customers get caught up in our culture because they want to believe there are still companies that trust their employees. We're always fighting the battle for belief, because onlookers are always looking for reasons to prove that trust doesn't work. But Armstrong will never abandon trust, even though we occasionally have setbacks, as the next story illustrates.

Points To Ponder From This Story:

1. Legends start when you dare to begin.
2. "You may have to fight a battle more than once to win it." Margaret Thatcher, former Prime Minister of England.

Armstrong Inventory Warehouses

This is a tragic story that began in 1994. This was the year we started a new manufacturing system which we affectionately call AMPS, which stands for Armstrong Manufacturing Planning Systems. It was not a tragedy that we went to a new manufacturing system, but it was a tragedy because our inventory accuracy was thirty-three percent when we needed accuracy of ninety-seven percent or better. To improve accuracy, we built warehouses with fences around the inventory. We appointed warehouse personnel who were the only ones allowed to remove inventory from their warehouses. Nobody else was allowed in the warehouses. In a short period of time inventory accuracy improved to ninety-nine percent.

One day Rex Cheskaty and I were walking through Plant Three. As we walked down the long aisle, Rex suddenly stopped. He jumped to the left and then to the right. Again, he jumped to the left, and then to the right. I looked at him with a startled expression and asked, "What are you doing?"

"Watch this, David." He jumped to the left again and said, "I'm in the warehouse." He jumped to the right. "I'm out of the warehouse." He jumped left. "I'm in the warehouse." He jumped right. "I'm out of the warehouse. Do you notice anything?" Rex paused . . . "We took down the fences around this warehouse!"

I smiled, "Yes, I see that now. Very good." Rex understood what makes Armstrong International great. Do you? If not, read on.

David's moral: *Self-management is not an act. It is a habit. To remain a habit, it must be practiced.*

Truly, I say to you that warehouses with fences will do more harm to Armstrong than inventory control at thirty-three percent. What do warehouses with fences say to you? To me, they scream, "We don't trust you! We can't count on you to keep our inventory accurate so we have locked it in a warehouse with a guard at the door." I would much rather see inaccurate inventory than have fences which remind people that self-management is not working. And I can hear the detractors already.

"Thirty-three percent!? See, you can't count on your people to manage themselves. They failed. You failed."

Maybe the problem was that we didn't communicate to employees exactly what accurate inventory was. Maybe they didn't realize the importance of putting inventory in its proper *location* so it could be found when needed. I believe every Armstrong employee understood good *quality*. But they may not have understood how important the correct *quantity* was to our inventory accuracy.

I approved the inventory warehouses to bring attention to the problem. Armstrong now recognizes and accepts its responsibility to teach everyone the importance of *location, quality* and *quantity* for accurate inventory. Our inventory accuracy is now at 99%, and I trust that every Armstronger knows the importance of inventory accuracy and will keep it at that level.

Will I remove the warehouse supervisors? As long as they provide a service to other departments, they will remain. But they won't maintain or enforce the accuracy of our inventory. That's the responsibility of every employee. Self-management keeps our quality superb. It gets our people to work on time and it's responsible for them making change in the cafeteria and for them not stealing from us. It will also, I trust, keep our inventory accurate.

Points To Ponder From This Story:

1. Warehouses with fences say, "I don't trust you."
2. I would much rather see inaccurate inventory control than have fences which remind people that self-management doesn't work.
3. You are just one <u>small</u> step away from losing your culture. Today a fence, tomorrow locks and next week time clocks.

Let's Make A Promise To ...

"Promises we can begin keeping right here, right now." *David Armstrong*

- Be giant.
- Practice self-control, which is always the best control.
- Lubricate our interactions with trust.
- Accept responsibility for our actions.
- Believe in ourselves and those around us.
- Be open, honest and trusting.
- Do the right thing because it's the right thing.
- Listen to our people.
- Not make exceptions.
- Agree that no action taken is too small - when it violates our culture. It's just the beginning.

David Armstrong

Chapter Five

"We The People...

of the United States..." Our nation's Declaration of Independence begins with the powerful word "We" in bold, passionate letters. Our forefathers understood the power of committed people. This country was built and has thrived for centuries because of its people. The same can be said of a company's quality—it begins with the people. I believe there was a time in this country when, for a lot of companies, quality was a goal to be pursued with frenzy and a prize to be displayed with pride. In the first family businesses, generation after generation learned quality and craftsmanship from their fathers and mothers.

Then came the assembly lines which reduced costs and lowered the price to customers. But at what price, I wonder? These same men and women who had learned the pride and satisfaction of carefully producing quality handcrafted products now found it difficult to be proud when the product was not theirs alone and when the family name was no longer on the line. The real tragedy is that today we are technically equipped to deliver the best quality in the history of the world. Complacency and greed probably have the most to do with why we don't.

At Armstrong International, quality comes from applying my seven S strategies for success (Swiftest, Simplest, Smallest, Spirit of Intrapreneurship, Surprises, Storytelling, and Smiles). Why do I want our products and customer experiences to be the end result of procedures, systems and attitudes which are the swiftest, simplest and smallest possible? Why do I want them delivered with a smile, a sense of surprise and the spirit of intrapreneurship (every employee acting like an owner)? Because every Armstrong employee knows that the job is not finished until the customer has an *enjoyable experience*—a quality product delivered in, around and through a quality encounter.

Southwest Air *Lives* Quality

For me, an enjoyable experience is a jewel with a thousand facets. The sum total of quality is the jewel itself. But it's built from every individual facet. Dull one or take it away, and you've diminished the brilliance of the jewel—and eroded its quality. Quality is only possible when every activity, no matter how small, bears on the final product. That's why Southwest Air, one of the most remarkable examples of quality and customer commitment in modern times, demands that their employees literally breathe superior customer service. "The mission of Southwest Airlines is dedication to the highest quality of Customer Service delivered with a sense of warmth, friendliness, individual pride, and Company Spirit." (1)

Did you read anything in that mission statement that depended on measurement of hard facts—like 95% on-time flights, no cancellations or overbooking and 2% or less luggage loss? No, of course you didn't. Because it's all about what I call the soft things—the enjoyable experiences. Generally speaking, friendliness at the counter and courtesy on the plane are rare for airlines. A smile and somebody who wants to help are all I ask. One time, on another airline, I heard an elderly lady ask a flight attendant for help to lift a bag into the storage compartment. What she heard was, "We can't lift bags. It's against company policy due to insurance claims from employees for injured backs." It was a small bag of about five pounds which I happily placed in the compartment.

One time a stewardess spilled milk on me and all over my computer. I didn't say a thing or even show disgust on my face. When she brought me some napkins, I said, "Thank you." I asked for a form to be filled out by the stewardess so I could file a claim in case my computer stopped working. She left and a few minutes later the head stewardess came to give me the form, but she said, "You know, sir, you should not be doing work on your computer while the plane is in the air." In other words, this whole thing was my fault. I had just given this airline $9,000 to fly business class around the world, a journey on which I was to make five stops. And this was the beginning of my trip. The only good thing was that my computer kept working, but I smelled like sour milk for the next 11 hours. No warmth or friendliness here, and it wasn't Southwest Airlines. So, please—no more lies while I wait for answers why my plane is late.

Quality is only possible when every activity, no matter how small, bears on the final product.

Yes, it's a mission statement. Yes, lots of companies have them. But the extraordinary success of Southwest is proof that theirs is more than a plaque to adorn the walls of corporate headquarters. Their 30,000+ employees are living, breathing animations of those 26 words. Last time I checked, that's the way it's supposed to be. The mission of a company ought to be visible each and every day in the actions of its employees. Each day provides the employees with a thousand little opportunities, which result in a thousand chances to impress customers with quality. Since these are little items and are largely spontaneous, the customer doesn't expect them when they come. That's how you change the perception of quality—by thousands of little reminders. It is often the little things that change things the most and last the longest. And every person on the employee roster, from the CEO to the freshest newbie, ought to model this behavior. If yours don't, then your mission statement is probably a wall hanging.

Quality is simultaneously the most talked about, sought after, misrepresented and overstated ingredient in business. Every company wants it. Every company says they have it. And maybe they do, because there are as many definitions and evaluations as there are firms defining and judging. The ambiguity that swirls about quality cannot hide the simple truth: American quality has fallen on hard times. In a global economy and marketplace, we no longer serve captive markets with the only game in town. As foreign competitors moved first into manufacturing and now into service sectors, they began to show us the face of the future and beat us at our own game. How have we responded?

Not well. Our comebacks lack energy, intensity, commitment and, seemingly, desire. We the people of the United States of America are still a *world-class* competitor. But in the loftiest spaces of business, finance, government and education, there seems to be an uneasiness about whether we can still muster what it takes to be *first class*. Our forefathers knew that winning freedom was all about commitment and passion. We can win the battle for lost quality, but make no mistake, it will require the same commitment and passion our ancestors showed in their unshakable belief in this great country and the willingness and desire to talk about it openly, honestly—like we used to.

"I pledge allegiance to the flag of the United States of America... ." How many young people of today can finish this statement of faith? How many adults? You probably last said it at the beginning of school each morning. For those of you younger than 35 years of age, I suspect you didn't know we started class each morning with: *"I pledge allegiance to the flag of the United States of America and to the republic for which it stands, one nation under God indivisible with liberty and justice for all."* The key word here is "I" which shows passion, pride, commitment and focus—focus on God. Oooops, we can't say that anymore. No more prayers in school. Wrong. You can always pray, just not aloud.

President Ronald Reagan was a proud American and a great storyteller. He believed we could do anything as a nation. Don't underestimate the need of other countries for this passion. If they get it, watch out, America. I have always considered great competition a benefit because it makes us better, which makes the world a better place for all of us.

The Lessons Of Lemons

An iron-willed poetry teacher played a starring role in one of the most colorful episodes in American product quality. Little did she know her quest for routine repairs performed fairly and in a timely manner would prove to be the first innocent step in a revolution. (Maybe she was a descendant of Paul Revere. Thank God his horse was sound and not a lemon.) Nearly 30 years ago, when Rosemary Shahan showed the courage to expect—no, DEMAND—quality and fair treatment, she ignited a firestorm of consumer wrath. After returning her car to the dealership following an accident, Rosemary got promises and not much else. Months later, nothing. So she picketed—and continued to do so in spite of torrential abuse, including insults, obscenities and gross gestures from mechanics. She unwittingly set in motion the popular outcry for lemon laws. Rosemary Shahan would go on to head Consumers for Auto Reliability and Safety (CARS).

CARS is a respected voice for the consumer's point of view and works tirelessly to spotlight illegal shenanigans, improve the safety of motor vehicles, and expedite the recall and removal of vehicles with dangerous defects before people are killed or injured by them. The group also is active in trying to stem the tide of "lemon laundering," the buying and selling of known lemons across state lines. Founder Rosemary Shahan has also served as a member of the Board of Directors of the Consumer Federation of America. It is the country's largest consumer advocacy group, embracing some 300 separate organizations with a combined membership of 50 million citizens.

For me, an enjoyable experience is a jewel with a thousand facets. The sum total of quality is the jewel itself. But it's built from every individual facet.

Three years after the start of her campaign in 1979, California and Connecticut put lemon laws on the books. (2) Today every state in the nation has some version of the lemon law. All states now have laws requiring auto manufacturers to pay a refund or replace a new lemon vehicle. Automakers produce millions of vehicles annually, so the argument goes, and a small percentage of so-called "lemons" is inevitable. Do you buy that? I don't— especially when you factor in the endless string of recalls. Recalls of both foreign *and* domestic makes, I might add. And I think lemons laws are a sad testimony to the erosion of product quality and reliability. It's a sorry day when the consumers must campaign for special laws of the land to protect them from a fundamental failure of one of our most prized industries. It sounds similar to taxation without representation, doesn't it?

Is It As Bad As We Think?

But wait a second. Can't automakers just start building better quality cars? Isn't that what started our slide down this slippery slope in the first place? Isn't others' plain poor quality the *real* reason why Toyota is the new Number One? And can't better quality save the day, even now? Well . . . maybe. As a matter of fact, some research *does* tell a different story, suggesting that maybe American cars are not that bad after all. An August 2006, news release from J.D. Power and Associates announcing its vehicle reliability findings had this to say about increasing quality.

"The gap in long-term quality between luxury and non-luxury brands has been cut in half during the past four years, according to the J.D. Power and Associates 2006 Vehicle Dependability Study (VDS).

The study, which measures problems experienced by original owners of 3-year-old vehicles, finds that there is an ever-smaller gap in reported problems between luxury and higher volume brands. Quality improvements with non-luxury brands are seen primarily in two categories—ride, handling and braking and engine and transmission—which both have a strong impact on customer satisfaction.

The presence of several non-luxury brands among the top-ranking brands in the industry further underscores the shrinking dependability gap between luxury and non-luxury brands. While Lexus is the top-ranking brand in vehicle dependability for a twelfth consecutive year and luxury-make Cadillac ranks fourth, three of the top five-ranking brands in vehicle dependability are non-luxury makes. Mercury and Buick, respectively, follow Lexus in the brand rankings, and Toyota ranks fifth." (3)

Perception Is Reality.

So why do many American buyers remain convinced that U.S. automakers put out inferior products? Remember, perception is reality, and a good many Americans have had a long time to see foreign-made vehicles leave ours in the dust. It's tough to quickly change those perceptions of bad quality. Fair or not, U.S. automakers seem to have developed a rep for poor-quality vehicles. And recalls don't help. They're a constant reminder. Problems affecting vast numbers of products leave a bad taste in the consumer's mouth and plant seeds of doubt. A buyer may not give U.S. makers the benefit of the doubt by going back to see how much they've improved when it's time to buy again. Again, perception is reality, no matter how old that perception is.

I have the right to expect to be satisfied—to have an enjoyable experience. I want to be rewarded for choosing a specific manufacturer, business or service provider.

"Perceptions about dependability can have a tremendous impact on an owner's satisfaction with their vehicle, which is not a small matter for manufacturers," says Neal Oddes, Director of Product Research and Analysis for J.D. Power and Associates. "In terms of retained value, recommendations and repurchase intent, and component replacement, vehicle dependability can have a direct impact on a manufacturer's bottom line." (4)

Other J.D. Power research sums up what I believe about quality and a quality (enjoyable) experience. Although this is describing banking, I think the point is entirely relevant to a host of products and services. "Positive experiences are a key contributor to advocacy and loyalty, and highly committed customers make more recommendations, use more products and services, and are more likely to positively impact the bottom line for their bank," said Jeff Taylor, Senior Director of the banking practice at J.D. Power and Associates. (5)

I believe that as a consumer, I have the *right* to expect to be satisfied—to have an enjoyable experience. I want to be rewarded for choosing a specific manufacturer, business or service provider. I want to get what I'm promised. I want to be treated well and fairly. And I want to walk away from the experience with a smile on my face and a good feeling inside. Why is this so hard for so many businesses to figure out? It's not just the product. Why do so many get it wrong when getting it spectacularly right is easier, better for business, provides more exercise for your smiling muscles and is just plain more fun?

Is Something Rotten In America?

How many times have you seen it? Someone will tilt their head back slightly, sniff gingerly and then pinch their face into a barely recognizable form. "Whoo-ee, something's rotten in Denmark." Well, it's not Scandinavia, and there may or may not be something foul afoot. Wait, I'll check my list of the latest recalls...

In testimony before a Congressional committee in May, 2007, Dr. David Kessler told lawmakers that the Food and Drug Administration (FDA) was in trouble. He should know. Kessler headed the FDA during the Clinton presidency. He said the FDA's food protection system is "broken," and lacks the funding, enforcement clout and modern scientific and regulatory infrastructure to provide adequate protection for the nation's food supply. He pointed to a constellation of other factors, including market globalization and the growing domination of FDA resources by its role as drug approval gatekeeper.

According to Kessler, the FDA is basically reactive in nature and is simply not equipped to be proactive in preventing food-borne illnesses. (6)

Food is just one more thing we can't seem to get right. It's in there with toys, consumer products of every description and, of course, automobiles. If you log onto www.recalls.gov, you can take a disturbing tour through the sobering world of recalls. They are grouped into major categories, including consumer products, motor vehicles, boats, foods, medicines, cosmetics and environmental products.

Is this the cost we must pay to live in a modern, fast-paced society? Is it the price of admission into a truly global economy and marketplace? I don't have the answers. But I just won't believe that quality and attention to detail have gone out of style. In fact, some would probably argue that from a *percentage* standpoint, tainted or failed products are a tiny fragment of our total output.

I want to get what I'm promised.

What bothers me most is the continual lowering of our standards of performance. We have reached a point, it seems to me, that the frequency of product shortcomings has dulled our sensibilities and muffled our outrage. Public acceptance, due to this repetition, has legitimatized inferior quality. Have we really reached a point where okay is okay? It seems to me to be a dangerous complacency.

An America of the dummies, for the dummies and by the dummies

One of the greatest threats to American quality may not be sloppy manufacturing, shoddy products or our increasing failure to protect our own food sources. It may be much deeper and far more worrisome. Let me illustrate with a story. An acquaintance of mine recently related an actual conversation with two graduates of a high school in a progressive state in the West. Try as he might, the young male graduate could not muster even one guess about who Abraham Lincoln might be. And when the conversation widened to the Civil War in general, he had no idea of why it was fought in the first place. His attractive female companion fared little better. When asked who won the Civil War, she scrunched her face up, examined the ceiling tentatively and then floated a trail balloon. "The West?" she tried hopefully. (After all, the absolutely stunning variety in lip gloss colors is so much more interesting than this boring stuff!) I can almost see her moving on to safer ground, ending the whole distressing episode with a flip of her shoulder-length blonde hair, a perky smile and a dismissive, "Whatever." True story.

During the 60s and 70s educational assessments conducted among the world's most industrialized countries showed that U.S. students placed a dismal last on nearly half (7 of 19) the tests. Furthermore, our students did not place first or second on any of them. In 1969-70 the first NAEP (National Assessment of Educational Progress), which reported progress by region of the U.S., showed similar results for 9-, 13- and 17-year-old youngsters. In spite of the poor showings, it was not until 1983 that the U.S. Secretary of Education published "A Nation at Risk." The report led to a number of reforms, including raising teacher standards, building support for better education at the highest national levels and improving school curricula. (7)

Although there are a host of factors contributing to the poor performance of our students, part of the problem may be a simple lack of focus. International research on mathematics and science probed the nature of the content in math and science curricula in 46 nations and what was expected of students. The examination showed that U.S. programs tend to cover far more topics but in less depth. For example, eighth-grade math students in the U.S. studied 30 to 35 topics. Their counterparts in Germany and Japan covered fewer than 10. The same is true of science, but it's even more lopsided. U.S. eighth-graders studied from 50 to 65 topics. Those in competing nations studied 15. It would seem that our teachers try to cover much more, but in far less depth. (8)

So focusing on less would likely get us more in terms of performance and retention. But, I believe there is something we should emphasize more in our curricula—finance. Our children need to be able to manage personal finances without Mom and Dad. And as the workforce of the future, they also need the ability to manage company budgets, read an income statement and handle balance sheets and cash-flow statements. I can't tell you how many times I have talked with someone who didn't know how to make and keep their money.

We also need to teach our children to communicate. I think everyone should take several speech classes if they hope to get promoted one day. One of the biggest fears people have is speaking in front of people—and that's not just big groups. A Speakers' Briefing at www.Americanspeaker.com offers valuable guidelines for public speakers. "A great speech focuses on Verbal Skills, Vocal Skills and Visual Presence. Verbal Skills (the actual words spoken) account for only 7% of the audience impact. So don't worry about being 100% accurate in the words you use. Practice more on how to deliver the message than on what you will say. Vocal Skills (your voice, tone, inflections, range vs. monotone, saying ah . . .) accounts for 38% of the audience impact. Visual Impressions (the way you dress and look, how you move on stage, stance and eye contact) account for 55% of the audience impact." You must know your audience and be confident and entertaining if you expect people to listen to you. Speak clearly and loudly, watch your tone, make frequent eye contact and be aware of body language, attire and speed of delivery.

We also need to nurture and train our imaginations. I find so little imagination in the general population and in the workplace. It exists with children but only until the ripe old age of six. Among the first things children hear when they enter school are these: *Color inside the lines. Stand in straight lines. Don't speak unless spoken to. Don't blow bubbles in your milk. Memorize and recite. The sky is not purple so repaint it blue.* Here is where creativity lives. But big changes occur after kindergarten. I fear imagination will always be in short supply because it is encouraged so infrequently. Yet it's exactly what we need to succeed as a country or company. Creativity is the springboard for new products, services and solutions to problems. So where's Creativity 101 and Intro to Imagination?

Let us not forget to add religion to our curricula. I remember when my son Kurt took Old Testament in college. He came home after several weeks and began to question the existence of God and the accuracy of the Bible. This all came from a college professor who turned out to be an atheist. This man had no idea what he taught. He didn't understand the law of non-contradiction, the law of cause and effect and why the word *chance* has no significance in explaining things. This man was protected by tenure so he would be difficult to remove. Is it any wonder why our children think the way they do? Fortunately, Kurt is a strong Christian today and well-grounded in doctrine, but he still has an open mind to listen to different people's interpretations of the Bible. Let's be clear. The Bible is 100% accurate. The problem is with our interpretation.

Yes, we should teach all these topics in college. I will end my list of suggested course additions with Entrepreneurship 401. I don't care if a student wants to be a doctor, actor, accountant or artist, he or she had better understand entrepreneurship. An artist, for example, who wants to move beyond pure painting to running an art gallery, will need to understand what it means to be an entrepreneur.

Asia Gets An A

The results of the 2003 Trends In International Mathematics and Science Study (TIMSS) are not encouraging. Eighth-grade students in Singapore, South Korea, Taiwan, Hong Kong and Japan topped the 40+ participating nations in combined math and science performance. For the younger students (fourth graders) Singapore, Japan, Taiwan and Hong Kong led the pack. (Korea did not test its students in this category.) U.S. fourth-grade students scored nine points above average in science and 11 points below in math. For American eighth graders, the scores were four points below the average in science and 24 points below in math. Don't believe me? How often have you witnessed a young person unable to make change when paying a bill? They can't do the simple math. Even if the cash register does the math I have found some unable to count the money back to me. They just hand over the cash all at once. Apparently, the more time our kids spend in schools, the worse they do. (9) This is not surprising when you consider the chilling scenario reported in a 2006 ABC News feature, "John Stossel's 'Stupid in America.'"

We must begin to apply the lessons of private enterprise and heed the strength of simple passionately held values.

Even though the report cites a Gallup Poll indicating that more than three quarters of American parents were relatively satisfied with their kids' schools, there is reason to believe that this may well be another example of famous American indifference. Or maybe it's an unwillingness to look too closely for fear of what we'll find. For example, when ABC wanted to send kids with video cameras into schools to show what's really going on, school officials balked. Requests for student-filmed sessions were denied time after time, state after state. And when they finally did get permission—at a Washington, D.C. high school touted as one of the best in the land—what they found was disturbing. One kid's video chronicled an unruly, undisciplined class where the teacher had no control. Another student-shot video starred a shirtless student in a wild dance in front of his teacher.

Much of the report focuses on the fact that American public education is a monopoly, and it points out that lack of competition usually destroys innovation and hampers progress. And to those who say it's all about money—or lack of it—the report notes that since the early 70s, education spending has swelled by 100%. Yet rates of graduation and achievement scores don't reflect an upward trend. Without competition, the report argues, there is little incentive to improve or excel.

It's hard to examine education without taking a long, hard look at teachers. But here too, the ABC report notes, the news is depressing. Contracts protect incompetent teachers. Once in, it's nearly impossible to get them out, apparently. Worse yet, the system shields sex offenders. In New York, a teacher sent sexually suggestive e-mails to a 16-year-old. Although he wasn't actually allowed to teach through six years of litigation, the system required the school to continue paying him, to the tune of more than $300,000, while it continued the battle to fire him. (10) "No surprise," you say. "It's happened before and will again." Again I ask: Have we grown numb by the sheer repetition of these events? Are we agreeing that okay is okay?

I'm no expert in education, but like any responsible American, I'm disturbed by anything that erodes our standards, threatens our security and diminishes our ability to compete, excel and deliver quality. Remember my example of quality as a jewel with countless "faces" or facets? We've been examining a few of them. Believe me, I know how easy it is to criticize, especially huge enterprises like the FDA or American education. But somehow we must begin to apply the lessons of private enterprise and heed the countless companies out there who have learned and daily take strength from simple values passionately held.

Self-Inspection

Three days had passed since Jim Bellew started working for Armstrong International, Inc., Michigan. It was his third evening when I first met Jim working the second shift.

"Hello, Jim. My name is David Armstrong. I want to welcome you to our family."

"It's nice to meet you," he answered. Jim quickly turned around as he put the next casting into the fixture to be machined.

"What do you know about quality?" I asked.

"In my previous job I was told quality is very important, that we should take pride in our work and only make a good product. I was also told I would be fired if I scrapped more than two pieces."

"Really?" I asked. "Was that for one day?"

"No, that was for one year."

"I'll bet you and the others hid your scrap so you wouldn't get fired."

"That's right," Jim laughed.

"Jim, that might be the way your past employer controlled quality, but passing bad quality to Armstrong customers will *really* get you in trouble. We understand that you will make mistakes and encourage you, no, DEMAND that you identify scrap and then find out why we have scrap. Don't hide it, thinking you're protecting your job. Sooner or later, someone will notice."

Jim asked, "That's really the way it is here, isn't it?" Jim then reached into a tray of good parts, retrieved a questionable casting he had machined earlier and put it into a tray marked "scrap."

"I'm proud of you, Jim. That's the way we do things at Armstrong."

David's moral: *A company's quality is known by its past reputation, not by its latest quality program.*

Employees need to learn from their mistakes. Armstrong learned a long time ago that a quality control department does not assure quality. We decided to make each and every person responsible for their own quality through self-inspection. (See my story "The Bluetag Special" in *Managing by Storying Around* for more details.)

As far as I'm concerned, the various "quality programs" which go in and out of favor are merely passing fads. While they offer the means to get you to quality, they do not *assure* quality. Only your people can do that.

I believe that a lot of these trendy "quality programs" spring from companies who have quality problems. If your company has good quality, don't lose it by blindly following someone who came up with the latest fix to solve their own short-term problems. Stay focused on what gives you quality, not the soup du jour. And remember, too, that just saying quality (or preaching it) doesn't make it so.

Points To Ponder From This Story:

1. Learn from your mistakes. Fix the "cause" of poor quality not the "effect."
2. "SPC," "ISO-9000" and "TQM" are new versions of a quality assurance department.
3. Popular new fads to improve quality come from companies with poor quality. They need to create a new image so they create these new programs. If you follow them, it is like the blind leading the blind.
4. Remind new people to self-inspect for quality. Don't assume they know.

Put Your John Hancock Here

*Y*ou're about to read a tragic story. When an Armstrong steam trap is finished in the trap assembly department, the Armstronger who assembled it must identify his work. Each assembler has his own special stamp that *only* he uses. He will take his metal stamp in one hand and with a heavy hammer in his other, strike it with a heavy blow, creating an impression of his personal mark on the product. This means he has checked the quality and it is good. The sign of a proud craftsperson. You do not want to miss the stamp and hit your hand. Believe me, I know! But that is not the tragic part of the story.

At Armstrong-Yoshitake, after an Armstrong water heater is assembled, a label is put on the heater. The person who assembled the water heater then takes a special ink pen and signs his name. The same is true of packaged water heaters where the fabricator signs his name and attaches it to the frame.

At Everlasting Valve in New Jersey, where the Everlasting boiler valves and specialty valves are produced, the employee signs his name on the paperwork for each valve.

If you happen to visit one of our Armstrong-Hunt plants, you will find the same pride in ownership demonstrated by the simple act of each worker identifying their work when building an Armstrong-Hunt product.

So where's the tragedy in this story? When one of *your* products is returned to the factory because of poor quality and your signature is on it.

David's moral: *Anybody can talk about quality; only those who have it can prove it.*—Dr. Deming.

"Good quality," says Tom Peters, "is a stupid idea. The only thing that counts is your quality getting better at a more *rapid* rate than your principal competitors." I agree. Improving quality in relation to our competitors is only good enough when we do it the quickest. That doesn't mean years or even months after our competition. And it doesn't mean days. Ohhh no! We must be the ones improving quality *before* competition. Quality is not an end point. It's not something you arrive at one day and then stop because you are done. Quality is a process—ongoing and never-ending. That's why it takes constant attention. By everybody!

Armstrong employees' putting their names on the line, so to speak, brings our concept of self-management and self-inspection to its logical conclusion. Without the willingness of our people to stand behind their work in front of our customers—and our trust in them to do so—the idea of self-inspection is hollow. Many of our examples are from the shop side of the business, but the idea of quality is just as relevant if you work in an office. Paperwork filled out incorrectly or sloppily is also evidence of bad quality. The same is true of poor phone manners, giving incorrect delivery dates or recommending a technical application that fails. Little things do matter. Even if they are the little bitty indicator lights you encounter in the next story.

Points To Ponder From This Story:

1. "If a man is called to be a street sweeper, he should sweep streets even as Michelangelo painted or Beethoven composed music or Shakespeare wrote poetry." Martin Luther King, Jr.
2. "Good quality is a stupid idea. The only thing that counts is your quality getting better at a more rapid rate than your principal competitors." Tom Peters
3. Armstrong employees put their names on the line.

Lites

I received a copy of a letter that a salesman had sent to his supplier (us), and at first I was pleased. "Things are going well in replacing the defective part on your product," the salesman wrote. "But I've noticed that the indicator lights are burned-out on 25% of the models."

When I looked into it, it was even worse. The failure was *at least* 25%. And this defect had been present since day one, and the product had been on the market for ten years.

"Why hasn't anything been done about this?" I asked.

"We've had other problems with the product that were more serious," I was told.

"Don't they understand?" I said to myself. What could send a louder message of poor quality than burned-out indicator lites on the front of our product? Our customers see these burned-out lights every day. That's a daily reminder of our poor quality. What is more serious than that our reputation is being damaged— daily.

The fact nobody was interested enough or willing to do anything about the problem shows they think some things are too small to be bothered with. But to a customer, that isn't the case. Customers perceive any problem—big or small—as something that should be fixed.

David's moral: *When it comes to quality, nothing is too small to be ignored.*

Okay, I admit it. I purposely misspelled the title of this story to see if you'd notice. I mean, it's only one word, right? And there are thousands—tens of thousands—in this book. So what's the big deal with one word spelled wrong? It doesn't really matter, right?

Wrong. Very wrong! Oh, there are other words misspelled and missing in this story. And maybe a typo here and there. I have obviously done it to make a point. Don't overlook something, even if it appears to be of little significance. You never know how someone will judge you. Did my mistakes in this story bother you? And you never know if your little "nothing" represents "the last straw" for a customer. To a customer, there is simply no such thing as a small problem. The operative word here is "problem." And if a customer has one—even a little one—you can bet it's a big deal to her. You should treat it the same way.

Points To Ponder From This Story:

1. **Little failures can lead to big failures. If you accept a little failure you are one small decision away from accepting a big failure.**
2. **To a customer, there is no such thing as a small problem.**

You Get What You Pay For—Or Do You?

Our company car may have been designed by listening to thousands of customers, have "advanced engineering" and have been voted Car of the Year, but you can't prove it by me.

After a long trip, I returned late one night to the West Palm Beach International Airport and walked out to my car. I opened the convenient tail hatch and threw my luggage in the back. I remember thinking how nice it was to have all this space for luggage.

As I pulled out of the parking space, I realized I had a flat tire. No problem, I thought. In ten minutes, I'd be back on my way. But then it hit me. I had never seen a spare in the car. Rummaging around in the dark, I found where it was hidden. Even better, I saw the jack.

The bracket holding the tire and jack to the car came complete with a T-handle to loosen the nut, which I thought was a great idea. As I grabbed the handle, I noticed it was cracked. My guess is a factory worker had over-tightened the nut, cracking the handle, when he attached the spare.

"Okay, David, just turn the handle slowly and easily, and it won't break." It broke.

There I am at 8 p.m. on a Saturday, 40 miles from home with a flat tire. I have a spare tire and jack but no way to get the tire free from the car for installation.

As I sat there fuming, I thought: "They talk about *quality*, but if they believe it, why didn't they make a better handle and why didn't the QA department catch the defect? More importantly, why didn't the factory worker replace the T-handle?

He had to know he cracked it by over-tightening. I mean, really… I could see the crack in the moonlight so the installer had to see it in a well lit factory."

Because the quality on a little thing was missed, I sat waiting for what seemed like forever for a tow truck to change my flat.

David's moral: *If you preach quality, practice it everywhere.*

If you preach quality, make sure you practice it—everywhere. People will judge your product by every part, even the handle that holds the spare in place. Quality is not just for the QA department, it should be the priority of every person who handles the product or deals with the customer.

Look to improve quality in a thousand little ways instead of through one huge technological leap. Your chances of satisfying your customer will be 999 times greater if you do. Poor quality is more noticeable in the small things which people use every day. Remember those indicator lights? The Japanese understand the big role of little things in quality.

Points To Ponder From This Story:

1. **Make quality everyone's number one priority.**
2. **Improve quality in a thousand little ways.**
3. **Quality (or lack of it) is more noticeable in the small things.**

Japanese Grocery Shopping

$\mathcal{I}$ had been told that in Japan quality is perceived by the appearance of the product. I discovered this was true when I decided to go grocery shopping in Tokyo.

The first aisle contained fruits and vegetables, and I immediately saw the pride in the produce come through in the packaging. The first item I looked at was a cantaloupe (perfect in color) with its stem extending three inches and tied with a decorative twist at the end. The cantaloupe was packed in a special container that allowed easy inspection. Next I looked at the strawberries. They weren't thrown into a pint container as they are here. Rather, they were each positioned individually within the box. All were bright red without a single imperfection. The onions had no skin fraying at the edges, and there was no dirt on them. The stems were individually cut for uniformity. The cauliflowers were small, but there were no brown spots to be found, and they looked as if they had been freshly picked and washed.

Over in the meat department, the famous Kobe beef was on display. Each piece of Kobe was perfectly sliced and presented on a tray made of *china*. The chicken was not piled up on a plate or placed several pieces to a package. Instead, each piece of chicken was in its own package. The window to the freezer case was clean. There were no fingerprint smudges or dust.

When I went to the checkout counter with my items, I was surprised to see there were no lines. There were two girls behind each counter—one to ring up the order, the other to bag it. They didn't use ordinary paper bags. Rather, the items were placed in a decorative paper bag similar to the kind you receive at an expensive store during the Christmas holidays. My shopping trip wasn't exactly like going to the local grocery store.

David's moral: *Quality is in the eye of the beholder.*

The Japanese perceive quality though a product's package, so the packaging and presentation are as good as they can possibly be. Imagine what their standards must be for items such as cars, computers, televisions and, of course, steam traps. It is *their* perception that matters. A company that is truly international adopts its markets' definition of quality, instead of trying to impose its own standards.

Points To Ponder From This Story:

1. Quality is in the eye of the beholder.
2. It is the customer's perception that matters—not ours.

Let's Make A Promise To ...

"Promises we can begin keeping right here, right now." *David Armstrong*

- Never rest until the customer has had an enjoyable experience through a quality encounter.
- Remember, quality comes from our people, not new programs/procedures.
- Put quality into everything: products, service, phone calls, paper work, packaging etc.
- Preach quality to new employees from their first minute on the job.
- Look to improve quality in a thousand little ways.
- Never forget that perception really is reality.
- Believe (and act as if we believe) customers have a *right* to be satisfied.
- Give 'em what we promise.
- Prove our quality every day, for it's a journey that never ends.
- Learn from our mistakes ... quickly.

Chapter Six

Give God a Job

God has a job at Armstrong International. In fact, He's always here, even when we're not. One of the many remarkable things about God is that He's always available and accessible to every employee who seeks Him in faith, on or off the job. All they have to do is ask. Wow. Talk about a model employee! I know He is able to help every one of us. But some choose not to ask for His help. Some of us know Him better than others. But probably few people have a closer relationship than Dan Lane.

I stopped in to see Dan recently, plopping down in one of the La-Z-Boy® chairs in his office. He was on the phone, so I sat looking around at his desk, the rows of books and the things adorning the walls. "Wow, if these walls could talk." I said when he finished his call. "I'll bet I'd have enough stories to fill a dozen books."

"Well, they may have talked once, but not anymore," Dan said, glancing about the room. "In 2003 they took an oath of silence. Nowadays, they won't repeat anything they hear—not even to the CEO. And neither will I," he added with a smile. Dan, you see, is the Corporate Chaplain of Armstrong International.

"David, I'm sure you remember that this office was the old corporate dining room." I nodded yes. One of the fixtures of my father's leadership was regular lunches with our employees. They were invited to join him on a random rotating schedule, enjoy a lunch prepared by our chef in this quiet, intimate setting. During the entire lunch hour employees could ask absolutely any question of my dad. It was a great way for him to listen, model our core values and to share his vision for Armstrong International.

"I can tell you a story about one of those sessions I had with your dad," Dan continued. I perked up at this. Mention of a story I haven't heard, especially one about Dad, always gets my attention. "You see," Dan went on. "The seeds for a Corporate Chaplain, which you made official, were actually planted by your father, right here in this little room." I sat back, ready to listen.

Planting The Seeds

"I was a brand new employee," Dan began. "I couldn't have been here more than a few weeks when I got the call to have lunch with Gus. When we met with him, I was struck by the impression of a man over-burdened. As your father answered each question, I began to reflect on what it must require to pull this off. What strength he must have to carry the weight of this company and its many employees on his back, day after day."

God has a job at Armstrong International.

"After the lunch, I called your dad's secretary and told her I wanted to see Gus. And all the time I'm thinking this is crazy. I'm going to get fired for this stunt. But I was so convinced that I was on the right track, I couldn't have stopped if I had wanted to. To make a long story short, I ended up in front of Gus again a short time later. When he asked me what he could do for me, I said, "Well, sir, it's really not what you can do for me. This is more about what I want to do for you. I want to pray for you." When I finished my little speech, he didn't say anything for a minute. He just looked at me with a mixture of surprise and anxiety. Here it comes, I thought. I'm a goner right here, right now."

"But Gus Armstrong didn't fire me. After what seemed like an eternity of reflection, he motioned for me to sit down. And for the next 45 minutes, he poured out his heart to this very green Armstrong employee sitting across from him. He told me about the frustrations, the disappointments, the hopes and anxieties and setbacks. He told me what was going well and shared his concerns about what might go wrong. He told me man-to-man—not company head to newbie employee—how good it felt to share with a fellow believer and how much he appreciated my desire to pray for him, his family and the company we shared."

"Well, David, that was 27 years ago. It is as fresh to me today as it was on the day it occurred. It was then that I started to pray for the Armstrong family and the family of Armstrong, so to speak. It was then that I began to understand that God had brought me to a special place. I didn't know then how He was going to use me, but I knew He had in mind a way for me to use the gifts He had given me."

"The seeds for a Corporate Chaplain, which you made official, were actually planted by your father."

Daniel Lane came to Armstrong International in 1979 as a draftsman. Not long after the experience with my father, in the early 80s, he sensed a call to ministry. He has since served as pastor at two churches, one in Sturgis, MI, and another near Battle Creek, MI. Dan probably would have gone on being a good draftsman and a devoted prayer warrior for Armstrong, but God used a personal tragedy to send him in a different direction. In 2000, Dan's son BJ died in a motorcycle accident.

Getting... And Giving Back

Dan has told me many times about the outpouring of support that flooded in from the Armstrong family and the extended family of employees and retirees. "I had people checking on me every day . . . and still do, in fact. I know what Armstrong did for me, and I wanted a way to give back if I could." Dan and I began to talk about a different role for him. In essence, we were discussing a Corporate Chaplain before either one of us really knew such a thing existed. We decided to try it on a trial basis. We put the word out, and Dan began spending half a day as a draftsman and half a day as a Chaplain for our people. It was clear from the start that we had tapped into a huge well of pent-up demand and need. We have an employee assistance program to help employees deal with crisis situations. Employees called on the program maybe half a dozen times a year. Dan was getting that many calls in a morning.

As I look back on the decision to create a full time Corporate Chaplain position from Dan's half-day experiment, I'm amazed that there was ever any hesitation about it. There was no shortage of opinions about what I should do, however. I knew what Dan wanted, of course. David Casterline, my Director of Corporate Communications, called me and said bluntly, "David, you need to approve this. It will be the most important decision you ever make as CEO." I told him I would pray about it and get back to him. Some thought it was silly. Some thought it would be seen as cramming religion down employees' throats. Others pointed out the potential problem of employees playing Dan against supervisors. *Too much gray area. Lawsuits waiting to happen. Hokey. Inappropriate for the workplace. People will laugh. We'll be the joke of the industry. Just plain unnecessary. Dangerous.* I heard all of these and more—and many of them from trusted, highly placed people whose opinions I respected.

In the end, the decision to name Dan Lane as the Corporate Chaplain of Armstrong International was an easy, peaceful decision. I looked at our history, the tradition of integrity of our leadership and our pedigree with employees and it all seemed to fit. Then I looked at our core values and our pride in the sanctity of our faith-based work environment, and the question was no longer, "Should we do this?" It became simply, "Why haven't we done this?"

As I look back on the decision to create a full time Corporate Chaplain position from Dan's half-day experiment, I'm amazed that there was ever any hesitation about it.

I'm proud to say that a number of good stewards correctly pointed out that 2003 was not a good time to do this. Times were tough. Business was down. They had every right to challenge the wisdom of creating another cost center, especially one as "unnecessary" as this one might prove to be. Wasn't it just window dressing, they asked. In the end, I made the decision for three reasons. 1) I'm a Christian, and Jesus has made it clear that I am to spread the Gospel and apply my faith everywhere – including the workplace. 2) I believed it would help the company create a better work environment, help employees at risk and reduce stress. 3) I believed it would differentiate Armstrong and help in our recruitment efforts. At this time I must point out that I do not use religion to make a profit. Some may accuse me of this, but anyone who truly knows me would never believe it. I truly believe that if we stay focused on God, He will provide for Armstrong in His own time.

The Might Of Being Right

By any measure, it has turned out to be the right decision. I agree with David Casterline. This really has been my most important decision as CEO. We now have a non-denominational chapel on-site in Three Rivers open to all employees, retirees and their families. With the help of Chaplin Lane, employees voluntarily organized regular prayer meetings, Bible study at noontime, and to date Dan has performed one marriage in the Armstrong chapel. David Dykstra and a few employees have organized an e-mail prayer hotline to multiply the power of prayer for friends and employees of Armstrong around the world. We have established a corporate Benevolence Fund, administered by Dan, to minister to the special needs of employees, their families and retired pastors and ministers. And best of all, some have discovered faith in Jesus for the first time through Dan's ministry.

Since establishing the Corporate Chaplaincy, I have been overwhelmed with expressions of thanks and gratitude. I have never had one complaint. Not one! On every visit to Michigan since the decision to make Dan's role official, I receive at least two or three and often a half dozen or more accolades. Employees write me notes, send me e-mails and stop me in offices and on the factory floor to thank me. It seems that they, too, believe that this was my most significant decision as a leader. And while some will call the three consecutive record years Armstrong has enjoyed since establishing a Corporate Chaplaincy a coincidence—you'll never convince Dan and me of that.

Dan's ministry is entirely non-denominational. You don't have to go to church to seek and receive his help. "I'm not trying to build a church," Dan is fond of saying. "I'm trying to build *the* Church." He always encourages those who seek him out to attend church, but he never pushes an employee to one church over another. And let's also remember that God's law will always be higher than man's law. He does not promote his role as much as he promotes faith in the workplace and the fact that you can't just turn off your beliefs when you walk into work in the morning. We want people to know that at Armstrong it is okay to have your faith in gear 24/7. I've lived through every step of this process, and I sincerely believe we've all been witnesses to how God is working among us—from the early lunch with my dad, to the way God used the death of Dan's son, to the remarkable response to Dan's role. Even the beginning of our chapel is a story of God at work. Dan tells it this way.

God's law is always higher than man's law.

"One day, I was unexpectedly overcome with grief and a profound sense of loss about my son's death. I just started looking for a place—any place—where I could get away and talk to God about it. I found myself in a storage room downstairs. It was full of junk and had just a single bulb dangling at the end of a cord in the center of the room. As I prayed and slowed my mind down, my eyes opened up to the possibilities of this little junk room. I went upstairs and e-mailed David. 'I think we need a chapel here, and I think I have found a place,' I remember writing. David wrote back, saying he'd be here in two weeks and for me to put together a plan and drawings for him to look at. I did, and he did—say yes. So you see, not only does God have a job at Armstrong, He has His own office, too."

Faith At Work

Faith in Christ is definitely on the move in workplaces across the land. Most observers attribute this bubbling up of faith initiatives in work environments to the self-centered, highly competitive and aggressive nature of life in today's world of commerce and the stresses and fears crystallized by 9/11. There is plenty of reinforcement, too, in the form of books, newsletters and organizations (Marketplace Ministries, Marketplace Chaplains USA, Corporate Chaplains of America, *Faith @ Work, Anointed for Business, God @ Work, Your Work Matters to God, Serving Christ in the Workplace, Faith & Work: Do They Mix?, Joy at Work* and *Jesus, CEO*.)

Co-mingling of faith and work is no stranger to the major corporations. In fact, one of the leaders is Ford Motor Company. The Ford Interfaith Network (FIN) has been around since 2000 and embraces employees of various faiths. The mailing list for interested employees is 5,000 strong. (1) Tyson Chicken employs more than 100 chaplains to minister to its employees. (2) Other well-known faith-friendly corporations include American Express, Ben & Jerry's, Hobby Lobby and ServiceMaster. Probably less well known is New Jersey's Atlantic Stewardship Bank, which tithes a tenth of its profits to Christian groups. (3)

While Armstrong has a Corporate Chaplain on staff, some companies outsource this function. For companies choosing this route, there are two major sources— Marketplace Chaplains USA and Corporate Chaplains of America. Marketplace Chaplains dispatches more than 1,600 Chaplains to some 250 companies in three dozen states. Although CCA is smaller with less than 100 chaplains, its stringent qualifications limit potential candidates. (4) Visiting employees in the hospital, conducting weddings and funerals, counseling about work-related issues and helping workers through personal crises 24/7 are all part of a corporate chaplain's role.

"I believe God called me to solidify the culture of faith here. And I believe He has given you the opportunity to impart much of importance."

Presently, Armstrong has only one Corporate Chaplain. Although employees company-wide have access to Dan, those at our Three Rivers, Michigan, campus clearly have the advantage of proximity. While I would like to eventually expand the number of our Chaplains on staff, we don't really have firm plans in place yet. We have attempted to hire another Chaplain, but each time we try we have encountered setbacks. I am reminded that God works in His time.

There is a predictable question here. It goes something like this: If the contribution of a Corporate Chaplain is so important at Armstrong, why doesn't he sit on the Corporate Executive Committee? It's a fair question. Dan, or someone in a similar role, may very well be a part of that group someday. Everyone on the Committee is there for a specific business discipline that they bring to the table. While Dan could certainly add a good deal, including opening our meeting in prayer, he would be out of his element, and quite honestly, I would be misapplying his talents and probably wasting his time by including him. He needs to be among the people, not in meetings. Besides, God is present in each meeting speaking to us—we just need to listen better. As long as we continue to live by our core values and keep applying the Golden Rule, I am confident that Dan will have a significant role in how Armstrong conducts its business. And he won't have to sit on the Executive Committee to do so.

Dan Lane is one of the giants at work I spoke about in another chapter. Gentle of nature and soft of voice, he once said to me, "I believe God called me to solidify the culture of faith here. And I believe, David, He has given you the opportunity to provide company resources and leadership. Remember, even when you are simply shaking hands, you are imparting something—your faith, your stewardship, the Armstrong legacy of integrity. And your stories can be vehicles to send the same messages. Never underestimate the power of a committed man driven by a powerful faith." It is a message—and an opportunity—I think about each time I share stories... like these.

Let's Pray

This story begins on the Internet. I had just downloaded my e-mail and was scanning though a list of letters when I found a letter from David Dykstra, Financial Controller for Armstrong Machine Works.

It was the end of the month and I wanted to see financials for that division so I clicked on his letter. I was surprised when I read the subject line in the e-mail. It read "Armstrong Prayer Hot Line." The letter was announcing the next monthly meeting for the Armstrong Prayer Hot Line. It just so happened that Tom Morris, General Counsel for Armstrong International, and I were in Michigan that week, so we decided to attend. Tom and I were pleased to see the number of Armstrong employees waiting for David Dykstra to lead them in prayer. "Let's pray," David says as everyone bows their head.

"Our Father who art in heaven, we pray to You today to give you all glory for You are the Creator and the Father. We **praise** You and worship You, and only You. We also pray to You to give **thanks** for the grace You have given us. And finally, we pray to **ask** for your help. We have many loved ones who are sick, who are in the hospital, who need your help. The families of these people also need your strength and guidance."

David then listed more than 20 names of people who needed a prayer due to sickness or deaths in their family. A few others in the group also gave a prayer of thanks and asked for help for their loved ones. After the last employee had spoken, David said, "In Jesus' name, Amen."

David's moral: *Prayer works because it strengthens us and our relationship with God.*

When you stop to think about it, prayer is a matchless gift. It has been given to us as a means of communicating with God. Just think of it—little old you and me having a one-on-one conversation with the Lord in Heaven. Make no mistake about it: Prayer is designed for our benefit, not God's. It is not the means of furnishing God with the knowledge of what we need. He already has that. It is designed, instead, as an opportunity to praise, thank and make confession to Him—to express our complete and utter dependence on Him for everything we have.

We can always depend on prayer. It always works because it strengthens us and our relationship to God. Prayer is a very personal way of communicating with our Heavenly Father. The more we communicate with Him, the better we know Him. In prayer, express **praise**, glory, worship and adoration. Give **thanks** for what He has given you—no matter how terrible things seem to be. **Ask** for things you need. He may not always give you what you ask for, but He always hears you. And He will hear if you ask for Him to deliver you from temptations like the one encountered in our next story.

A Point To Ponder From This Story:

1. **Prayer is designed for our benefit, not God's.**

Lead Us Not Into Temptation

On a cold Sunday morning, the Reverend Dr. Dale Kent told our congregation a story with such passion that I wanted to share it with you. It has a great deal of meaning for me.

"My first day at college brought me face-to-face with my roommate, who happened to be a Native American. As we talked, he told me a story about a Native American boy who was entering manhood.

"To prove he was worthy of joining the rest of the men in his village, the young man decided to climb to the peak of a very high mountain. He put on a deerskin shirt, covered himself with a blanket and started his journey.

"After a great climb, he finally reached the top, and as he looked out he said, 'I can see the whole world.'

"Just then, he heard a noise below his feet. He looked down and saw a rattlesnake. The boy was just about to jump back when the snake said, 'Please, don't leave. I'm very cold, and there's no food to eat. Please put me under your shirt and take me down the mountain.'

"'I can't,' said the boy. 'I know what you are. You're a rattlesnake. You'll bite me and I'll die.'

"'No, I promise,' said the snake. 'Please take me where I may live in warmth and find food to eat.'

"The boy, with goodness in his heart, decided to take pity on the rattlesnake. He put the snake under his shirt and headed down the mountain.

"When he reached the valley, he placed the snake on the ground. As he did, the snake struck, biting the boy on the wrist.

"'You *promised*,' said the boy just before he died. 'Why did you bite me?'

"'You knew what I was,' said the snake. 'You knew what you were doing.'"

David's moral: *You don't lie, cheat or steal off the job. Why would you do it at work?*

Your basic sense of right and wrong is not something you can switch on and off at will. It doesn't work that way. You can't check your sense of right and wrong at the door or put it on hold temporarily. Morality exists twenty-four hours a day. We deal with temptation every day. Just consider what happens at work. We are surrounded by temptations to steal product from the factory, steal time, falsify an expense voucher or take office supplies home. Like the boy in the story, we are constantly tempted, and we know what we are doing.

At Armstrong, those in need will find help is available if they only ask. If employees need a loan or want to borrow tools to finish a job at home, help is a question away. All they have to do is ask. They will likely receive what they need from co-workers or the company. They have no need to take what they would probably be freely given if it was requested. Although temptation makes <u>choosing</u> right from wrong hard sometimes, <u>knowing</u> right from wrong is easy. That's because, as the next story reminds us, God gave us a blueprint for building a moral, God-honoring life.

Points To Ponder From This Story:

1. Don't check your sense of right and wrong at the door.
2. Temptation is everywhere. Be alert.
3. Don't give in to temptation. Ask for what you need, and you will likely receive it.

The Ten Commandments

Long, long ago there was a wise man named Moses. One day Moses climbed a mountain called Mount Sinai. When he reached the top, he was on holy ground and God spoke to him, giving him Ten Commandments on two stone tablets that people must follow.

I.   You shall have no other gods before me.

II.   You shall not make for yourself a graven image.

III.   You shall not take the name of the Lord your God in vain.

IV.   Keep the Sabbath Day holy.

V.   Honor your father and mother.

VI.   You shall not kill.

VII.   Neither shall you commit adultery.

VIII.   Neither shall you steal.

IX.   Neither shall you bear false witness against your neighbor.

X.   Neither shall you covet your neighbor's wife, house, fields or anything that's your neighbor's.

These commandments were cast in two stone tablets.

David's moral: *Good stories are worth much. Good stories retold are worth much more.*

Retelling stories, whether they are about religion or your company, is crucial to keeping them alive. The stories which bring life to historical facts and legends are always just one generation from extinction. If one generation fails in its duty to keep telling the story, it will be lost. It is not the objects or events that we pass on to our children. It is the stories of these things that are our heritage. Without the story of Moses climbing Mount Sinai and God writing the Ten Commandments on stone tablets, the tablets become just stone. The same is true of Armstrong (and your company). They become simply piles of bricks. Unless you read "Our Promise to Fred Kemp" in my book, *Managing by Storying Around*, you have no appreciation of why plant three is located where it is. Its location means nothing just like the two stone tablets - without a story.

Make no mistake . . . remove the story from the event or object it relates, and it loses it significance. Each generation must tell the story as accurately and as often as possible or the next generation will say, "There was once a man named Moses who climbed a mountain—I can't remember the name of the mountain—

and God gave him the Ten Commandments on stone tablets. The Ten Commandments said:

I.   You shall have no other gods before me.
II.   You shall not make for yourself a graven image.
III.   You shall not take the name of the Lord your God in vain.
IV.   Keep the Sabbath Day holy.
V.   Honor your father and mother.
VI.   You shall not kill.
VII. Neither shall you commit adultery.
VIII. Neither shall you steal.
IX.   Neither shall you bear false witness against your neighbor.
X.   Neither shall you covet your neighbor's wife, house, fields or anything that's your neighbor's.

The next generation will tell the story, "There was once a man named Moses who climbed a mountain—I can't remember the name of the mountain—and God gave him the Ten Commandments on stone tablets, but I can't remember what they said. By the third or fourth generation, the story will go, "There once was a man—I can't remember his name—who climbed a mountain and he received some stone tablets with commandments on them from God. I can't remember what God said or how many commandments there were, but I hope the story will help us keep our faith." This is why stories must be faithfully retold. If they are not, we forget details—essential facts that make the stories powerful and effective.

Points To Ponder From This Story:

1. **It is critical to retell a story to keep it alive.**
2. **It is not objects or events that we pass on to our children. Stories are our real heritage.**

The Chapel

Imagine yourself walking down the steps near the front office and into another world. You pass through a wooded area with stone walls bordered by beautiful trees. Geese fly high overhead in a "V" formation. Far below is a lane that leads to Lake Armstrong. As you continue, you pass a water fountain of angels with water flowing gracefully from their hands toward Mary and her newborn son Jesus.

To the right is an old wrought iron gate with a sign that reads, "Coram Deo." It begs you to enter. "What does this mean?" you think to yourself, as you stand before the door with your hand on the knob ready to enter through the gate. Why would this sign be on this door?

You open the door. Immediately your senses take in a beautiful scene: colored crushed velvet curtains, a slate floor, a ceiling that resembles a tent. There are wrought iron knot tables, one with a candle flickering upon it. Placed on the table is a memory book to record the name of loved ones who have gone on home before us. You see beautiful oak pews; stained glass windows; candelabra with three candles, symbolizing the Father, Son and Holy Spirit. You admire a portion of Michelangelo's "Creation" painting and hear soft music playing from somewhere in the sky.

You have just entered the newly dedicated Armstrong Chapel.

David's moral: *God has an office at Armstrong.*

God's room at Armstrong is a place of solitude, quiet and beauty. It is available for anyone who wants or needs to spend a few minutes enjoying this wonderful place provided by a family who puts God squarely in the center of its business. Feel free to use it anytime. Take advantage of an opportunity to get closer to God for He truly knows your heart.

Points To Ponder From This To Story:

1. **God is always present at Armstrong.**
2. **You can visit His place of solitude, quiet and beauty while at work.**

Let's Make A Promise To ...

"Promises we can begin keeping right here, right now." *David Armstrong*

- Give God a job in our company.
- Pray for each other.
- If we are Christians, let it show in how we conduct our business.
- Bring our faith to work.
- Pray because it strengthens our relationship with God.
- Remember that temptation makes choosing right from wrong difficult, but knowing right from wrong is easy.
- Never check our sense of right and wrong at the office door.
- Tell and re-tell the stories of our faith and our company, so we won't forget who we are.
- Give God an office at our company.
- Read the Bible which contains 365 commands to "fear not." I believe this is the most repeated command in the Bible. This is to remind us <u>daily</u> that we will face hardships that provoke fear.
- Believe God will not wink when we sin. Not even for the sake of good business.

Chapter Seven

Service Sells It ... Every Time

In the middle of the 1950s, milkshake machines were the latest in the string of things Ray Kroc had sold since he quit school to hawk coffee beans. He later worked as a jazz musician, sold Florida real estate and peddled paper cups. By 1954, Kroc was 52 years old, weary and still looking for his first big break. Little did he know he'd come face-to-face with it the day he aimed his car into a drive-in burger joint in San Bernardino, CA. The place was run by Richard and Maurice McDonald.

The McDonald brothers were hauling down about $350,000 a year by selling a few basics from a nine-item menu. Their secret was in the speed, efficiency and uniformity of their "Speedee Service System." A born salesman, Kroc immediately saw potential and convinced the brothers to franchise the system. By early in 1955, he had his own version of the West Coast McDonald's up and running near Chicago in Des Plaines, IL. Four years later, he had more than 100 stores in operation. In 1961 Ray Kroc bought the whole shebang from the McDonald brothers for $2.7 million. Five years after this, he was worth more than $35 million and well on his way to global expansion. In 2005, McDonald's had 31,000 stores worldwide. (1)

They acted like they were glad you were there. What's more, they looked like they were enjoying their work.

Yes, it was only burgers and fries, but here was simple and inexpensive food that tasted good and was reliable. No confusing menus or snooty waiters that made common folks feel uncomfortable. This was America's restaurant, affordable enough that even a family of modest means could eat out occasionally. I'm told in the early days, the speedy, polite service from clean-cut (mostly male) workers was a marvel to watch. They were polite and enthusiastic. They acted like they were *glad* you were there. What's more, they looked like they were *enjoying* their work, and the place was spotlessly clean, gleaming stainless steel and all. Going to McDonald's was an enjoyable experience.

Changes In McLand

Stop by a Mickey D's today, and things are likely to be a little different. Oh, the food will be familiar enough. The Big Mac is still holding its own, as it has been since its debut in 1968. And the Quarter Pounder? Yep, still there. Going as strong as ever since arriving on the McDonald's menu in 1971. Even the procedures are vaguely familiar. After all, they haven't changed much since Ray Kroc drafted The Manual in 1958. (2) But gone are the days of a simple nine-item menu. There are dozens of choices nowadays. Want breakfast? Choose from lots of variations. And you can get salads, yogurt, pies, cinnamon rolls and parfaits. Depending upon where you are in the country, there may be special region-specific choices as well. Under fire in recent years for the nutritional value in its offerings, McDonald's has had to respond and change. And following in the footsteps of change has been variation in the well-honed model that made the chain famous for speed and efficiency. Gone are the days of seamless uniformity. The McDonald's of today is a different animal than its perky predecessor.

But many would say that McDonald's needed to change to keep up with the times and one step ahead of critics who were criticizing the chain for its high-fat menu items. In a world that worships choices, having your way instead of McDonald's way had to come sooner or later. So things have changed. And the ingredient in the recipe for success that has changed most dramatically for every fast food chain is service. Now, I'll admit I don't spend a lot of time in fast-food outlets, but I've had enough exposure to them to be aware of some extraordinary lapses in service—and a serious erosion in the quality of the customer experience.

The McDonald's of today is a different animal than its perky predecessor.

I don't use those popular drive-thrus, primarily because of all the people I see parking and coming back inside with a drive-through order gone astray.

Something is missing or something is wrong too much of the time. And I watch all of this while I'm *standing in line* waiting for service on the inside. The clean-cut kids that used to dominate the ranks of fast-food workers are few and far between nowadays. Mostly you'll get lazy counter persons in wrinkled, dirty uniforms. Often their hair is uncombed and their eyes are clogged with the crusty by-product of sleep. Depending on their bulk, they either waddle or shuffle through the routine, often with an attitude that suggests they're doing you a favor by paying you any mind at all. The clothes are baggy. The shirts are half in and half out. They yawn open-mouthed while taking orders. They don't listen. They don't pay attention. They don't care. As often as not, they're trying to weigh in on a gossipy exchange with co-workers, dividing their attention between this distraction and the needs of the paying customer. What happened? Fast-food restaurants used to provide the quickest service of any restaurant in town . . . and at affordable prices. Today, there are many—even sit-down restaurants—that have faster service, and the prices are the same but with a better atmosphere and cleaner restrooms. These fast-food eateries used to be a vast training ground for eager youngsters aching to serve. In fact, one estimate from the early 90s suggests that seven percent of American workers can thank a McDonald's restaurant for their first job.

Outrageous Service Or Outraged At The Service?

I've actually approached a fast-food counter where no fewer than five staffers were slouching in idle chatter. No one moved to help me. I waited. No one moved. Finally in exasperation, I stretched out both arms with palms up in a plaintive "what gives here" gesture. When I see things like this, I want to leap over the counter and grab the manager in one hand and the nearest loafer I can reach in the other and crack their heads together or shake them until their teeth fall out. "Don't you know I *chose* your restaurant?" I want to yell. "Of all the places that line this street, I picked this one. Now reward me for that decision. Show me you care. Treat me like you appreciate my business. Do something that will make me want to come back. Your job is to treat me well and send me away happy. Why can't you get this?" Outrageous service is not an act or a game. It is a habit. Bad service comes from bad habits. (That's why I want to wring that manager's neck.) Make sure your work habits are modeling service and quality. Yes, I know I've spent a lot of time harping on fast-food service, but I've done it for a reason.

Actually, for a couple of reasons. First, these places used to be where young workers entering the workplace learned about service. You never forget your first love or your first job. And second, my experience tells me that what's happening here is spreading. The same kind of attitude and service are creeping into mainstream restaurant chains and other service businesses who employ young workers.

If you haven't guessed, service is a hot button for me. It's no coincidence that one of the very first stories I ever told in that session with Tom Peters more than 20 years ago was about service. It was an engaging story about the simple act of an unassuming young waitress who was focused on her customer and looking for any way she could to make a positive impression, meet his needs and send him on his way, pleased and smiling. Some of the best, most attentive service I've ever enjoyed has been dispensed by those who have the least—and the fewest reasons to go the extra mile. They are products of an environment where service began at home. Parents' lessons began at home and at an early age. As parents, we used to nag, repeat over and over, tell story after story, set rules, give tasks to complete and show examples to our children about how to behave. Some still do, but unfortunately, too few. These early lessons became a part of the moral fiber of these young men and women. They become focused on the things you taught them—like respect for authority, hard work and, yes, great service. It is not about intelligence, education or experience. It is about the attitude and pride which they learn from you and me as parents. Pay attention to your children so they will grow up learning to pay attention to others.

"Don't you know I chose your restaurant? Of all the places lining the street, I picked this one. Now reward me for that decision. Show me you care."

The world of tradesmen seems to be especially bad when it comes to service. Often skilled tradesmen work alone or have very small companies with few employees. So you'd think delivering great service would be easy, right? Wrong, very wrong. When friends gather and the talk turns to home repairs, the stories get ugly. One friend remembers when he wanted to replace the furnace in his home. He called four companies. Two never responded to his calls. A third came and looked but never followed through with an estimate. The fourth got the job. Maybe Woody Allen was right. A big percentage of life *is* just showing up. Most of us can recite similar stories about plumbers, carpenters, roofers, painters and so on down the line. I live in Florida where we've had damage from several hurricanes. I can't cite too many examples of outrageous service, but when it comes to outrageous stories about lack of service and price gouging, ask Florida residents trying to get hurricane damage to their homes repaired.

A Very Bad Idea

Trying to arrange home repairs or dealing with problems at the office share some common frustrations. But the worst on both fronts is the dreaded phone tree. As far as I'm concerned, it stands alone at the top of the list of the World's Worst Ideas. And it has probably done more damage to outrageous service than any other single development. To add insult to injury, often the people you do manage to connect with can't or won't help you. One customer of a high-tech company claimed that a customer service rep, a supervisor no less, laughed at him before hanging up. In an interview with a St. Louis newspaper, a former Customer Service Representative (CSR) for a major cable supplier said, frustration about technicians showing up on time was number one among the 100 to 125 calls she juggled daily from unhappy customers. You've never had this happen to you - have you? Have you ever noticed how happy you are when somebody actually shows up on time? This is the new standard of service, and we endorse it with a smile. I guess Mom and Dad forgot to teach these technicians the pride of showing up on time. Even though CSRs had no idea of where the techs were or when they might show up, they were directed to tell the customer that all was well and the cable guy would arrive as scheduled. It was a lie. They were not allowed to transfer calls to a higher authority because sending more than seven percent of their calls would get them written up and disciplined.

Although a major computer maker touts its 24/7 award-winning service, customers often find something far different after the sale. ABC News reported recently that a major computer seller in the U.S. is having customer service problems serious enough to prompt a lawsuit by the New York Attorney General. (3) Maybe the bigwigs at this company are out of touch with what really happens in the customer service trenches. That's sort of the bottom line of a survey reported on The Red Tape Chronicles, an online feature of MSNBC.com. According to the feature, a recent survey among CEOs of high-tech companies indicated that the guys at the top believed the companies they headed were delivering customer service that was "above average." As if that's good enough. Their customers think differently, with 60 percent of them noting some degree of dissatisfaction with how their service requests were handled. The net result is likely to be a former customer: more than 80 percent of those who believe they've been treated badly report they'll buy elsewhere next time. On the other hand, companies who take the time to put their house in order and improve service will be rewarded with customers who are very loyal and very willing to buy from the same company again.

But Research Says I'm Wrong

That's right. Despite what you and I have heard, seen or experienced, the numbers (at least some of them) tell a different tale. The American Customer Satisfaction Index is a national economic indicator of customer evaluations of the quality of products and services available to household consumers in the United States. It is updated each quarter with new measures for different sectors of the economy replacing data from the prior year. The overall ACSI score for a given quarter factors in scores from about 200 companies in 43 industries and from government agencies over the previous four quarters. The index is produced by the University of Michigan's Ross School of Business in partnership with the American Society for Quality and CFI (Claes Fornell International) Group. But I have to ask: Are people really "satisfied" with what they're getting? Or have they simply resigned themselves to the fact that what they're getting is as good as it gets? Have they dropped their expectations so low that average is now the new standard? I have my answers. You'll have to come up with yours.

A February, 2007 news release said, "Customer satisfaction with the goods and services that Americans buy reached an all-time high in the fourth quarter of 2006, according to a report released by the University of Michigan's American Customer Satisfaction Index (ACSI). The 74.9 ranking on the ACSI's 100-point scale is the highest score the index has had since its first measure in 1994." Lest you grow giddy at such news, let's not forget that 74.9 is a long way from 100 and still only a "C" in laymen's terms. Remember, too, that this was an overall score representing a cross section of industries.

If we look at the airline industry separately, we see that it racked up a score of 63. This represents a two-point decline from its 2006 score of 65. Of the industries surveyed, only the cable and satellite TV industry ranked worse at 62. The airlines' 63 score is even lower than the satisfaction rating for the IRS which is 65.

The first employee a customer encounters will probably determine the future relationship between your company and that customer.

Customer satisfaction with the retail sector, which includes department and discount, specialty retail stores, supermarkets, gas stations and health and personal care stores, rose 2.8 % to 74.4 on the ACSI's 100-point scale. . . . The department and discount stores industry is one of the industries that did not improve this year, slipping 1% to 74. But I say again, in my view a rating in the mid 70s is average at best—a sobering placement for a nation that prides itself on being the best in the world. If we accept this we are doomed.

By May, of 2007, ACSI reported that customer satisfaction with the goods and services that Americans buy continues to improve, but at a slower rate. . . . The ACSI is up 0.3% to an overall score of 75.2 on the ACSI's 100-point scale, the highest quarterly national average in the ACSI's 14-year history. However, although customer satisfaction growth in the aggregate continues, the rate has slowed and many individual companies measured this quarter are falling behind. Of the companies measured in the first quarter of 2007, the ACSI saw more drops than gains in satisfaction.

"In addition to the large numbers of decliners, the rate of improvement in satisfaction has slowed," said Professor Claes Fornell, director of the University of Michigan's National Quality Research Center, which compiles and analyzes the ACSI data. "Companies don't have much pricing power unless there is shrinking supply or higher customer satisfaction. There are no signs of the former in most industries, so the latter becomes more critical. Companies may begin to see narrowing profit margins unless there is further improvement in customer satisfaction." (4)

Remember, the employees who have the greatest potential for giving great service are the ones who have the greatest motivation to make it a priority. Employees closest to customers are the first to discover problems. Listen to them. Better yet, empower them to deal proactively with problems and deliver service to customers. The first employee a customer encounters will probably determine the future relationship between your company and that customer. Make sure your people have everything they need, including the necessary authority, to make sure that first impression is a positive one. Think about an entire company moving in unison to deliver outrageous service. Well, now. That could be a wonder of the modern world. Let's go back to my first story ever told.

Sweetened Iced Tea

It was a hot day in July. A salesman, Jon Bingaman, and I had just finished making a sales call. While driving to our next appointment we decided to stop and get a cold drink. We pulled into a truck stop restaurant. I ordered an iced tea.

"Could you bring me some Sweet'N Low™ with that, please?" I asked.

"The sugar is on the table," smiled the waitress.

"Yes, but it doesn't dissolve in iced tea as well as Sweet'N Low™ does."

"I'm sorry. That's all we have."

When the waitress came back with our drinks, she placed a small metal cup down next to my iced tea. "I'm sorry we don't have any Sweet'N Low™. So, I took some hot water and poured it over some sugar to help dissolve it. I hope that's okay."

Now that's service!

On the way out, I went up to the waitress and gave her a $2 tip for my 60-cent iced tea, and I thanked her for the best service I'd had in a long time. You should have seen her co-workers' expressions. Ask yourself; was it the $2 tip or my public praise for a job well done that startled her co-workers? Maybe both. I must have told this story over fifty times.

David's moral: *There is no such thing as a commodity. Everything - even a glass of iced tea, can be differentiated with service.*

Wow. I still remember that waitress. She stands head and shoulders above most of the so-called service I encounter today. Good service should be everywhere and be absolutely unaffected by geography, function or business category. Remember, I received this service in a truck stop. A truck stop! I've had less attentive service in five-star hotels and restaurants. At Armstrong (and your company) customers should experience great service in every department, not just sales.

Truly good service is rare, so reward it whenever you find it. If you see colleagues providing exemplary service, praise them. If you receive outstanding service, do everything possible to encourage it. In this story, I deliberately made a big deal of the excellent service the waitress delivered so I praised her in front of her peers and gave her a 300+ % tip. This was a wonderful example of solo service, but sometimes (often, in fact) good service takes teamwork. Such is the case in the next story.

Points To Ponder From This Story:

1. Serve others as you would want to be served.
2. I don't define service. You don't define service. The customer defines service and that's all that matters.
3. Reward great service.

"You Want It When?"

𝒯his story has a happy ending, but you wouldn't have thought so, given the way it began. It began with a problem. A big one!

Our Armstrong-Yoshitake plant had been unable to ship some orders because a key part was not in inventory. Armstrong-Yoshitake prides itself on having the fastest turnaround time in the industry (standard delivery time for these orders is three days) and the orders were now several weeks old.

Tom Rockwell, the sales specialist who had sold the order, decided to see what he could do to help get the shipment out the door. He went to see the foreman Gary Vedmore.

"Gary, what's the problem?" Tom asked. "The order should have shipped weeks ago."

"We're swamped," frowned Gary. "There's just no way we can get to it for another couple of weeks."

Tom knew that was unacceptable, so he asked if he could machine the parts himself and finish his office work later. Gary had Bill D. Hartman, a machinist, show Tom what to do so he wouldn't get hurt. In addition to doing his own job that day, Bill kept checking to see that Tom was okay.

Tom was fine. He made all the necessary parts that day, and the orders went out the next morning.

David's moral: *Everyone, including the boss, must be prepared to drop everything to satisfy a customer.*

If you say an order will ship on time, do everything in your power to make it so. *Keep your word.* If everyone knows that the number one job is satisfying customers, it changes perspectives and reshuffles priorities. In this story, making the parts was more important than anything else Tom might have done in the office that day.

The real hero of this story is teamwork. Tom helped Gary. Bill Hartman helped Tom. These men made something happen. They didn't wait for an overseer to take charge. They looked at the problem and came up with a way to solve it. They *did* something. To Tom's customers he *is* Armstrong-Yoshitake, and the company's reputation is entwined with his willingness to take action and solve problems. Always remind your employees that, when dealing with customers, they *are* the company. Certainly, the customers are important. But are they more important than making time for the boss? The Armstrong answer is in this next story.

Points To Ponder From This Story:

1. Customers usually don't view companies as a bunch of buildings and a mailing address somewhere. They see companies as the people they deal with.
2. I promise! Two powerful words that can make or break you, and not just you, but also your company. Keep your promise. Be careful what you promise.

Rush Job

*D*on English, Assistant Foreman, Armstrong International, Inc., Michigan, told me he didn't have time to talk to me, the CEO, one morning. It all began when I received a message that Don wanted to speak to me. I had already tried twice that week to talk to him, but both times he was gone. On my third visit to his department I found him hard at work welding a manifold. I waited until he was finished, then interrupted him.

"Don, I have a message you want to speak to me."

"It wasn't that important. You didn't have to get back to me this quickly."

"That's okay. When I'm in town I like to take care of my messages so people don't think I forgot."

"David, I hate to say this, but I can't talk right now. I've got this rush job and we've got to get it out today. I've already spent eight hours on it and I'm going to need two hours of overtime just to finish it. Could you come back later and talk to me?"

I smiled. "That's no problem, Don. I'll come back tomorrow and talk with you when you have more time." I continued my journey through the shop.

David's moral: *He who wishes to secure the good of others has already secured his own.*—Confucius

An owner wouldn't have a company without the customer, so the customer is always number one. And if the customer comes before the owner, then the customer comes before *everyone* in the company. Did Don English make a mistake in telling me to come back later? NO! I took pride in the fact that he sent me away so he could service the customer.

"That's what got you to the position of Assistant Foreman," I told him, "and that very same attitude will make you Foreman one day." If you want more people like Don in your company, you have to spread the word and make them a positive example for other workers. I made sure the message was clear by telling others how proud I was of Don. And I wrote this story to share with you what it takes to get promoted at Armstrong.

I made a big deal of thanking Don for his actions, but my thank-you pales in comparison to this one...

Points To Ponder From This Story:

1. **Do you consider it a privilege and not just your job to serve the customer? Maybe if you did you would go that extra mile and tell the boss you're too busy to talk.**
2. **Know when to speak up. Don't let a title like CEO scare you from servicing the customer.**

Valentine's Day

𝓣he sound of a violin could be heard as I approached the building. When I opened the doors, the sweet notes were bouncing off the walls. There in front of me stood a man in a black tuxedo with a red carnation. In his hand was a violin, and I watched as he drew the bow across the strings. Out of the corner of my eye, I saw some people watching. I turned and noticed two people I had never seen before leaning against the wall listening. Then my eyes drifted toward the reception desk of Armstrong Service where I saw Donna Sealy and Janette Vazquez listening to the music with smiles on their faces. Donna and Janette each held a red rose. I looked up to the second floor and saw ten or twelve Armstrongers listening as the violinist played his song. With a few minutes, the song ended and the man took his violin from his chin.

Donna and Janette then turned to me, "Good morning, David. We'd like to introduce you to Gail Hines and Joe Bellow from AmeriSuites."

"Good morning, Mr. Armstrong."

"Good morning. You're from the hotel we often use for our seminars and out-of-town guests, aren't you?

"Yes, sir. We are very thankful for your business. Come visit us soon."

I started walking to the conference room when I looked back and once again saw the red roses Donna and Janette were holding. Then I remembered: It was February 14—Valentine's Day.

David's moral: *A thank-you should be memorable.*

AmeriSuites knows that getting new customers is difficult—and their elaborate thank-you proved they understood that keeping a current customer is more important. AmeriSuites already had most of Armstrong Service' business... and they wanted to keep it. The in-person thank-you, complete with red roses and a violin said in a very memorable way that they valued our business. Here's another example of superb service—less flashy, but just as outrageous.

Points To Ponder From This Story:

1. AmeriSuites knew whom to serenade for future business ... and it wasn't the CEO or President of Armstrong Service, Inc.
2. Say thank-you with style. When saying thank you, look the person in the eye. If you're real brave, sing them a song or play a violin.

It's Only A Box

A couple of weeks ago Gary Cebulla, one of our Armstrong Factory Ambassadors, sent me his laptop to update his ACT database and to do some maintenance on it. I had sent him a **"Special"** Laptop Shipping Box that costs Armstrong $30.00. Mailbox, Etc., guarantees the computer will not be damaged and UPS has an extra guarantee when these boxes are used. Obviously, I did not want to be responsible for any shipping damage. I arranged with Gary the best time for him to be without his computer. He informed me that he was out of the office until that Friday and wouldn't need it until then.

The computer arrived in perfect shape. The box was in great shape, too. I would be able to reuse it for shipping the computer back to Gary. I thought I was putting the box in a safe place (an empty office).

All updating was complete. The laptop was working better than ever on Thursday morning, just in time to be shipped back by the Friday deadline. As you have probably guessed by now, I went to get the **"Special"** box and it was gone! I searched high and low. I checked all trash areas, cleaning room areas, recycling areas and even had Rich Wright, one of our maintenance personnel, check the recycling container outside. Unfortunately, the container had been emptied earlier and all the materials were gone.

My last idea was to call the cleaning company, ServiceMaster, to see if they had thrown the box away or knew where it was. They informed me that they had recycled it the night before. Mike King, the manager of ServiceMaster, clearly heard the disappointment in my voice. I informed him I had made a promise to get the computer back to our customer and now I would need to make a special trip to Kalamazoo to get another box (I know it's only a box, but it was a **"Special"** box.) to get it shipped out that day. Mike told me not to worry. He arranged to get another computer shipping box and drove it down to Three Rivers by the 1 p.m. shipping deadline. The computer shipped that afternoon and—as promised—arrived at Gary's front door on Friday.

David's moral: *Since you are the company, service starts with—you guessed it—YOU.*

This story came from Pam Blasius, and here's why I'm very proud of her. In her story, she refers to Gary as the customer. She knows that Gary is a fellow Armstrong employee, yet she treats him like a customer. Pam gets it. And so does that ServiceMaster manager who went the extra mile.

A Point To Ponder From This Story:

1. **Brand your culture; it takes time – lots of time. I've preached that customers include fellow employees as well as paying customers. Today, I see more Armstrong employees treating each other as customers, but it has taken over a decade to make this our culture.**

Let's Make A Promise To ...

"Promises we can begin keeping right here, right now." *David Armstrong*

- Go the extra mile. Deliver outrageous service. The only question is what is outrageous? My answer, we can't be too outrageous.
- Show we care and that we value and appreciate customers and their business.
- Reward customers for choosing our company with a caring *attitude.*
- Learn the difference between paying money and paying attention.
- Listen to the employees who are closest to our customers. They will be the first ones to spot problems.
- Make sure our people know that the first employee a customer encounters will likely determine their relationship with our company. Why not the second or third person, you ask? The first person has already set the tone for the others to follow or overcome.
- Demand that every department, not just sales, delivers outstanding service.
- Reward great service and apologize for poor service.
- Make sure every employee knows the number one job is satisfying the customer.
- Make service memorable with *Enjoyable Experiences.*
- Keep our word.
- Treat fellow employees as customers.

David Armstrong

Chapter Eight

The Shrinking Power of Globalization

Under the cover of darkness, grim-faced men and women dart about, walking with brisk determination over a rain-slicked tarmac. The hope of a fragile world rests on the slim chances of an extraordinary plan. Scientists on both sides of the Cold War have mastered miniaturization. The only catch is that it's short-lived, and objects that have been made small by shrinking their atoms quickly regain their original size. Now, the only man on earth to know the secret to overcoming the problem lies near death. Unless something extraordinary can be done quickly, a blood clot in his brain, suffered in a CIA-engineered escape from the Other Side, threatens to steal the secret forever. So a desperate plan to save his life takes shape, and technicians prep a group of scientists in a submarine for miniaturization and injection into the professor's body. Their mission: Get in, destroy the blood clot and get out—in one hour!

Okay, that's not *exactly* what we mean when we speak of our shrinking world. But that was the premise of the 1966 film *Fantastic Voyage* starring Stephen Boyd, Raquel Welch and Ed O'Brien. Do you remember? Based on the novel of the same name by Issac Asimov, it was another in a seemingly endless string of films from moviemakers who delight in playing around with the relative size of objects. The trick, you see, is to either make people little or other creatures big and then sit back and watch the fun. (1)

Smaller Or Flatter?

Technological advances, *are* shrinking the world. Technology doesn't really change our world physically, of course. But it does alter our ability to see the world we live in more completely and to a greater depth. Of course, what we're talking about with all this shrinking-world code is globalization—blending, merging, combining. The standard elements, events and experiences of life are becoming more connected, similar and integrated.

As early as 1999, three-time Pulitzer Prize winning Foreign Affairs columnist for the New York Times, Thomas L. Friedman, chronicled globalization in *The Lexus and the Olive Tree*. In a new book, *The World is Flat: A Brief History of the Twenty-first Century*, he shares a phased vision of globalization. Friedman sees the world presently in what he calls Globalization 3.0. Globalization 1.0 occurred from the age of the great explorers until after World War I.

This first stage was the globalization of nations—when great nations colonized large parts of the globe—shrinking it from large to medium. The second phase, Globalization 2.0, took place from after World War II to the year 2000. This was the globalization of companies. It shrunk the world from medium to small. Friedman calls the present Globalization 3.0 the globalization of individuals, and he says it is shrinking the world from small to tiny. The result of all this? According to Friedman, the outcome is a flattening of obstacles for people everywhere, which permits individuals and small groups to live, work and prosper in a new global village.

Technology doesn't really change the physical size of our world. But it does alter our ability to see the world we live in more completely and to a greater depth.

Many forms of technology have been working for decades to make the world smaller. I think it's helpful to look at this as a tandem process. On one hand, there is a constantly increasing volume of information. And once we have access to it, information simplifies things. It takes the mystery out of them and makes them suddenly approachable. In addition, there are technologies which make it easier, more practical and more efficient to disseminate and communicate about what we know. Information replaces mystery with comfort and familiarity. It removes the anxiety about the unknown and opens our eyes to the potential of the known. Think, for example, of what a revolution the printing press was. Instead of scribes copying manuscripts, machines could record information, duplicate and share it. Every stage of history has played its part and made its contribution to this process.

Even Bronco Charlie had a role. On a sunny July day in 1861, this feisty 11-year-old leapt onto the back of a pony and sped out of Sacramento, CA, and into history as the youngest Pony Express rider. One of the most colorful chapters in the story of communication, the Pony Express wasn't really intended as a long-term form of mail service. Its backers wanted to draw attention to the central route (St. Joseph, Missouri, to Sacramento, California, by way of present-day Kansas, Nebraska, Colorado, Wyoming, Utah and Nevada) in the hope of winning a rich government mail contract. For a short while, it *did* provide the fastest mail service between St. Joseph and Sacramento. The service began on April 3, 1860, when young $100-a-month daredevils on ponies began relaying mail by riding day and night through every season. Traveling about 10 miles an hour, riders got a new mount about every 15 miles and rode between 75 to 100 miles before turning the mail over to a fresh rider. In summer, riders could cover the nearly 2,000 miles in about 10 days. Winter trips took anywhere from 12 to 16 days. Until the telegraph officially ended the experiment in October, 1861, the Pony Express was the fastest communication between east and west. (2)

Technology doesn't really change the physical size of our world, of course. In the 1860s, moving mail across 2,000 miles of forbidding terrain in 10 days probably seemed remarkable. Today, it seems laughable because we know so much more and our modern options for communicating what we know have changed our perspective. We say the world is smaller because Missouri and California seem closer together, owing to all that we know and our many choices for connecting and communicating.

Technology Expands Our Knowledge

Today, the pace at which we create and communicate information is almost incomprehensible. In fact, some of the measures for the volume of our knowledge are beyond comprehension, at least mine. The last half of the twentieth century saw a remarkable list of advances that multiplied our technological progress. Computer and software breakthroughs transformed information technology, and the Internet knit the world together in a global neighborhood. Medicine marveled at the development of the CAT scan and MRI imaging. Reconstructive surgery and replacing many parts of the body with highly advanced prosthetic devices are now commonplace.

In the field of energy, we saw the development of nuclear power, solar power and new battery technology. In transportation, refinement of the jet engine and the growth of commercial aviation made it easy and affordable to rub shoulders with our fellow citizens of the world. Transistors reshaped our world for all time, and they have made possible much of the technological flavoring of the life we now enjoy—inexpensive home computers, global air transport, cell phones and other consumer electronics and non-invasive medical tools—to name a few. (3)

The standard elements, events and experiences of life are becoming more connected, similar and integrated.

In 2003 the School of Information Management and Systems at the University of California at Berkeley conducted the *How Much Information 2003?* study. Its findings include the following:

- The volume of new information stored on various media, including paper, film, magnetic and optical, is estimated to have doubled from 1999 to 2002.
- Various media produced approximately five exabytes of new information in 2003.
- Instant messaging produces an estimated five billion messages each day or 274 terabytes each year.
- Email creates an estimated 400,000 terabytes of new data per year.
- Worldwide phone calls accounts for an estimated 17 exabytes of new information

If you're like me, all these bytes are more than I can chew, let alone swallow. So let's get a little context. A byte is eight bits representing one character in a computer's memory. Bytes are units of measure for file sizes, computer memory and space on hard disks. A kilobyte is about 1,000 bytes. A megabyte consists of about a million bytes. A gigabyte is a billion bytes, and a terabyte is about a trillion bytes. But it doesn't stop there. The complete list for measuring computer data is as follows:

1. byte
2. kilobyte
3. megabyte
4. gigabyte
5. terabyte
6. petabyte
7. exabyte
8. zettabyte
9. yottabyte

Just in case you were wondering, a yottabyte is 1,208,925,819,614,629,174,706,176 bytes. For reasons that are completely beyond me, the measures actually increase by 1,024 instead of 1,000, but the terms are usually estimated by multiples of 1,000. That's why earlier, I said that a kilobyte was "about 1,000 bytes." (4)

But you're probably still thinking, *But what do these things mean? Relate a kilobyte, for example, to something I can understand.* Fortunately, the folks who put that Berkeley study together oblige. According to them, here are some rough equivalents that make them easier to understand.

Two kilobytes	One typewritten page
One megabyte	Small novel or a 3.5-inch floppy
One gigabyte	Pickup truck filled with books
One terabyte	50,000 trees worth of printed paper
Two petabytes	All academic research libraries in U.S.
Five extabytes	All words ever spoken by human beings (5)

Armstrong's global brand is known as the Four Es—Energy, Environmental Emissions, Enjoyable Experiences and education.

Any discussion of globalization has to recognize the issue of outsourcing or "offshoring." There's no doubt that in the process of shrinking, the world has sucked countless jobs out of the United States, first manufacturing spots and now, increasingly, service positions. There are many opinions on both sides of this discussion, and whole books have been written on this aspect of globalization alone. Thomas Friedman believes that the last thing we should be doing is erecting walls. He points out that the driving force behind our economy has been our ability to innovate and he sees it as our mainstay for the future. I agree. Remember when I talked earlier about the need for imagination and creativity to be taught to our children? He also points out that in 1900, fully one-third of our workforce labored in agriculture. Today, it is a fraction of that, because an innovation-fueled economy has absorbed those workers into other segments. (6)

Benefits Of Globalization

Even the harshest critics of globalization would find it hard to ignore some of the undeniable benefits of a shrinking world.

- The percentage of the populations of developing nations living below U.S. $1 per day has been cut in half in just two decades.
- Since World War II, life expectancy has increased threefold in the developing world.
- Universal suffrage in 1900 was largely nonexistent in developing nations. By 2000, it was a fixture in more than 60% of the world's nations.
- In the 1960s more than half of the world's population lived in nations where per-day food supplies provided less than 2,200 calories per person. By the 1990s, the figure had dropped to 10 percent.
- Global literacy rose from about 50% in 1950 to more than 80% in 1999. Literacy among females as a percent of male literacy rose from less than 60% in 1970 to 80% in 2000.
- Children as a percent of the labor force fell from about 25% in 1960 to 10% in the year 2000.
- Growing numbers of the people in the developing world have access to clean water and enjoy increasing availability of autos, radios, electric power and telephones.

What's more, solving many of the problems facing the world today requires the combined efforts of a community of nations. Air and water pollution, global warming, damage to the natural environment, threats from international terrorists and regulation of outer space are all challenges demanding international cooperation and collaboration. (7) (Armstrong's global brand is becoming known as the Four Es—Energy efficiency, Environment, Enjoyable Experiences and Education.

- About 99% of the world's 6.5 billion people are in developing nations.
- For the first time in history, the majority of the world's populations live in cities.
- As of 2003, 25% of the world's population had traveled by airplane. More than 500 million of them flew on international flights.
- In 2002 16.6 million Chinese tourists traveled abroad, topping the number of Japanese travelers for the first time.
- In 2002 China made the study of the English language in grade school mandatory.
- As of 2002, India was the number one film-producing nation with 1,200. The U.S. ranked second with 543.
- The number of people in developing nations who are 24 or under is now larger than the entire population of the world 50 years ago.
- The 84 million residents of the Philippines send a daily average of 2.4 text messages per citizen—some 200 million per day. (8)

It's not as if we can really choose to embrace or ignore globalization. It is here. It affects how we earn our livings, the food we eat, the clothes we wear, the machines and devices we use for transportation, communication and entertainment. So if you want to try to go it alone, good luck. But you might as well join the rest of us in gathering up the fringes of our comfort zones and repeating all together, "One, two, three—stretch."

The world seems to be growing smaller and changing in every way imaginable. Here are some stories to help you understand how changes in The World have meshed with the world of Armstrong.

Do You Speak English?

$\mathcal{I}$ remember once being halfway around the world in the country of Thailand. While listening to Larry Daugherty's presentation on Armstrong's Flo-Rite Temp® water heater to our sales representative (Alpha Group Company Ltd.), I was asked to visit with the managing director. Mr.

Somboon had a large notebook on a conference table. When I sat down, he handed me a fax from Armstrong Machine Works. The fax notified Alpha Group Company of a partial shipment, and this concerned Mr. Somboon. He then slid a piece of paper across the table to me. It was their purchase order, and he pointed to shipping instructions. It said "No partial shipment." As I read the Armstrong fax again, it was obvious that some of the product had already been shipped. Even though the handwriting was clear, I re-read the fax several times to make sure I understood the message correctly. I did. It was Armstrong's mistake. I agreed to solve the problem by paying the additional freight and extra duties due for the partial shipment. But then I asked a more important question.

"Mr. Sanboon, do you always receive answers to your faxes in handwriting?"

"Oh, yes. That is very common." He opened the large notebook and revealed several past faxes, all in handwriting. "This is a problem for us, for many times we cannot read the handwriting because it is so sloppy. You don't even use a reference number. Your people just write an answer on our fax and send it back."

I reviewed each fax and could tell that some were very difficult to read. Not everyone's handwriting was clear. While flying home, I had 26 hours to write this story. I have witnessed this kind of poor communication many times in the past. The following will help establish a new policy for all Armstrong International divisions when communicating with other countries.

David's moral: *Justifying a fault doubles it.*

It really is true: Everybody speaks English. All the business people in all the countries I've visited have spoken English and have wanted to practice speaking English when I was there. It's sad but true that we Americans, with few exceptions, are too lazy to learn another language. We always justify this by saying, "Everybody speaks English, so why should we learn a new language?" The first thing we must do is change our attitude—not about learning a new language, but our willingness to improve the way we communicate in our native tongue, English.

Remember back when you were ten years old. You were learning to speak and communicate on a simple level? You used small words of only a syllable or two, not three or four. You also wrote in short sentences. You used very few adverbs and adjectives. You might be wise to use that same basic, grade school English when communicating with our sales force and customers overseas. If you have ever tried to learn a foreign language you know the past and future tenses are tricky. Be careful not to use past or future tenses but rely on present tense most of the time. Proper grammar is not as important as clear communication. It's rude and arrogant to speak quickly when someone is trying to translate. Speak s-l-o-w-l-y and repeat yourself often using different words. As Americans we may not speak several languages but we can make it easier for those who are trying to speak English by practicing the above.

Points To Ponder From This Story:

1. **Everybody speaks English, but can you read your doctor's written prescriptions? Make sure your writing, better yet printing, is legible. Printing is much closer to computer keys and more recognizable.**
2. **Use simple, grade school English with small words and short sentences. Keep it in the present tense.**
3. **Speak slowly, giving your audience time to translate.**

The Seven Wonders of the World

𝕱ar, far away in a distant land is where this story begins. We had just built a new manufacturing plant in Beijing, China. During our stay over the weekend we had a chance to see one of the Seven Wonders, the Great Wall of China. About twenty Americans from Armstrong International piled into the company bus. We rode in that bus up and down hills for about an hour. As we got off the bus, the driver gave each of us a cold Coca-Cola.

With our Coca-Cola cans in hand, we began to walk the steep steps of the Great Wall. Sometimes we would stop and look down the side of the wall, commenting on how long it must have taken to build. The wall was over fifteen feet high. What caught me by surprise was the thickness of the wall. I expected a tall but thin wall. Actually, it was wide enough for two cars to drive on it side by side. The steps were very difficult to climb—very steep. It was quite a workout. Slowly you could hear the Coke cans—pssssh, psssh—as people opened them to take a cool drink. Halfway through the trip we stopped to have our pictures taken on the highest point of the wall. That's when I saw one of our Armstrong members set a Coke can down on the wall and leave it. I'm sure it was by accident, but I took no chance.

"Don't forget your Coke can," I whispered. "We shouldn't litter—especially at a national treasure."

"Oh, I forgot I put it here," was the response as he quickly went over to pick it up. Shortly afterward we found wastebaskets for our empty cans.

David's moral: *Consider yourself an ambassador for the United States and your company*.

Like it or not, you need to face an important reality: When you or your employees travel, you do so as ambassadors of your country and your company. The citizens of the country you're visiting take notice of every action you take and every word you speak. Make sure both reflect positively on your country and company.

One of the United States' most valuable brands is Coca-Cola. Littering a national treasure with a Coca-Cola can harms that brand image and could even endanger jobs and business relationships. Remember, you are an ambassador in all you do. One important way to prepare for that role is to learn all you can about the laws of the land you are visiting. Be familiar with the customs, conventions and taboos. Knowing and following these local traditions shows respect.

Points To Ponder From This Story:

1. Ambassadors of the United States and _____ (Fill in the name of your company) do not litter a national treasure of a foreign country.
2. Only brands last forever, except when used as litter.
3. Know the laws of the land you are visiting.

Wood Screws

*F*ar, far away in a land where our day was their night, and their night was our day, stood a new factory for Armstrong International. Kangsen-

Armstrong's offices stood four stories tall with a manufacturing plant across the courtyard. Surrounded by a wrought-iron gate with its own security tower, it was a sight to behold. To promote the Armstrong products, Kangsen-Armstrong built its own seminar demonstration facility. Armstrong International sent two working ambassadors to help install the new facility. Rex Cheskaty, Corporate Director of Technology Development, and Ed Kirschner, Maintenance Manager, came to build a demonstration facility second to none in China.

While Rex and Ed laid out the blueprints to review, they noticed Mr. Li, Technical Seminar Supervisor for Kangsen-Armstrong, taking apart the wooden crates that held the seminar equipment. With his screwdriver he carefully removed each wood screw and placed it on a piece of cloth. Rex and Ed watched Mr. Li as he put one wood screw after another on the piece of cloth until finally they became bored.

Later that day work began on installing the equipment. As they positioned the trap boards, they looked for some fasteners that must have been shipped with the equipment. After searching the crates, they found no fasteners. They decided to make some phone calls. Surely in a city the size of Beijing, they could find something. After many phone calls, it became apparent that this was going to more difficult than they had thought. It could take days to find the proper fasteners.

Suddenly, Mr. Li realized the situation and tapped Rex on the shoulder. He then placed the piece of cloth in Rex's hands and unfolded it, revealing all the wood screws. At that point in time, those wood screws were worth their weight in gold!

David's moral: *Wise men don't need advice. Fools won't take it.*—Benjamin Franklin.

Although Rex and Ed are certainly not fools, they were not wise men in China. They made an incorrect assumption, based on their life and experience in the United States. In China there are no handy Home Depots or Builder's Square warehouses brimming with all the things we Americans take for granted. Live and learn.

Since labor is so abundant in China, the extra time Mr. Li took to remove all the screws was not expensive. Looking for wood screws and then paying for them would have been more expensive than the extra time it took to carefully remove them. When you're working in other countries, remember what resources they have before making decisions. Don't decide using the same logic you would use back home. You'd be making a huge mistake not to recognize, understand and leverage local knowledge. You may be well financed, have the best technology and unlimited manpower, but you will probably fail if you don't tap into the power of local knowledge which creates a *local* common sense. And we all know how far common sense goes in resolving problems. Do not underestimate local knowledge. What seems foolish to us may be very wise in your host country.

Points To Ponder From This Story:

1. **Be resourceful. A case in point: Wood screws are more scarce than labor in China.**
2. **Local knowledge is power.**

Male or Female

ere's a story to make you laugh. There once was a foreign woman filling out an application for a job in the United States. She filled out her name, street address, last place of employment, and then came across the word sex: _____. This was confusing to her because in her own country one can tell if an applicant is male or female by their name. Also, she had heard that Americans were very open and uninhibited about sexual matters. So she filled out the form as follows: "Sex: Twice a week."

David's moral: *Foreign travelers beware.*

If you have not studied the customs of the country you are to visit, you're in for trouble. For example, one custom when eating in China is to leave a little food on your plate when you are full. In America, we have been taught just the opposite—to always clean our plate. If you clean your plate in China, they will keep putting food on it because it means you are still hungry. So if you want to "project what you are" and be taken seriously as an international traveler, know the customs of the countries you're visiting.

Points To Ponder From This Story:

1. **"Failure to prepare is preparing to fail."—John Wooden**
2. **"It is a fact that you project what you are."—Norman Vincent Peale**

Roger's Story of Heroic People

*B*elieve it or not, in the year 1982, Belgium's unions declared a strike. The industrial park where Armstrong International, Belgium was located, and local companies FN, Cockerill (steel mill), Memorex, Colgate, Burroughs and our neighbor across the street, Danly, had strong unions so they also went on strike." Roger Closset, Plant Manager for Armstrong, Belgium, takes a drink of coffee and continues his story.

"Back in 1982 we had no problem at all in the beginning of the social movement, but after several weeks, Armstrong was the only plant working in the Hauts Sarts area. We were, of course, smart enough to have very few cars on the parking lot; most of our people were parking their cars at the Post House Hotel and walking to the plant. I also made several trips to pick up people.

"Nevertheless, our office and factory were invaded one day early in the morning. The group leader was a socialist union leader, a very tough guy. Some employees came to work while the strikers were blocking the office entrance. The people tried to stop them and force them to stay outside, but one secretary was so upset that she pushed the men and entered the office. While walking to her place, one tried to make her fall. She immediately reacted by pushing the man aside and went to her place. At that moment, the rough guy came to her, took her typing machine and raised it up, threatening her with it. She was not scared and told him to keep cool and that he had no right to forbid her to work if she so wanted. Then an office employee intervened, and everybody cooled down and could finish the day's work. It was for her a question of principle and respect of each individual's freedom. We were, however, told that we were not allowed to work the next day.

"The next day all office and shop employees were at work and very soon we were invaded by about 30 people, many of them women, who were the most aggressive. Some of them went directly to a secretary, accusing her of being on the employer's side and trying to convince her to fight against the employers. She, of course, expressed her own arguments and ideas, and after a while the group left the office rather mad. She reported that she never thought that human beings could show so much violence, aggressiveness and hate as she saw in the eyes of those women while talking to her against her bosses.

"After many talks and personal contacts with the mayor of the town (a friend of mine, although Socialist) and with the State Policy, we decided to stop working for security reasons. Only management people were allowed to stay at work. I had about 10 managers in the office during that period! The strike was at its height and the employees (not all of them) were really mad because of what they could read in the newspaper and see on the TV news.

"When I came to work at 6:00 a.m. the next day, the entrance was blocked by a few cars, and the strikers were across the street. I drove through the yard and parked my car as I normally do in front of the office. No other car was on the parking lot.

"I put the lights on in all of the offices and started the computer. It was, of course, absolutely quiet. Suddenly, I heard some noise coming from the shop. I was surprised but also afraid. I still had in mind that years ago the building next to Armstrong burned completely overnight while being occupied by employees who were on strike.

"When I pushed the door to the shop open, I was really surprised to hear the noise from machines. There were four people at work: our maintenance technician, a machine operator, a trap assembler and a humidifier assembler.

"They told me that they could not accept being fired by outside people and that if some had the right to strike, they had the right to work. They arrived at 3:00 a.m. with one car. They parked far away from the factory on one small road, put the car on jacks, removed one wheel and installed the legal red triangle. They crossed the field and entered the plant through the back door. They left at 11:00 a.m. in the same way. The other people who didn't act in the same way didn't lose any money since they worked extra time to recoup the hours they were forced to lose.

"Although we were disorganized during a couple of days, we *never lost one hour of production because of a strike*. It is still true today, after almost 25 years. To understand the context of this story, one should be aware of the strength of the unions and of the social climate in Belgium. Laws are created almost to force people to be unionized. For example: In the metal industries, the employers have to pay one social contribution to one solidarity fund whose goal is to pay additional indemnity in case of a long period of sickness. For unionized people, they get their money from the fund after a reduction of 15 percent for *administrative cost*. We once had the same case with one of our non-unionized shop workers, and we paid the 15 percent difference.

"In case of unemployment, it is well known by everybody that you get your social security money very fast through unions. This creates support for the unions.

"For the others, it is more complicated since they have to go through a public office and this can take quite a while.

"This is the reason why we at Armstrong have decided to quickly pay our non-unionized workers for unemployment, and we recover the money from them after they are paid by the public office. That's Armstrong International, SA!"

David's moral: *You're only as good as the people you hire.*

The risks these employees took make their story even more memorable. Few people would have assumed such risks, but then few people are Armstrongers. They showed how much they cared about the company, and the company will not forget it.

Points To Ponder From This Story:

1. All countries have fair, honest and hard-working people.
2. "In the middle of difficulty lies opportunity."—Albert Einstein
3. No noble thing can be done without risk.

Let's Make A Promise To ...

"Promises we can begin keeping right here, right now." *David Armstrong*

- Use technology to expand our knowledge and capability.
- Embrace a smaller world as a bigger opportunity.
- Use simple grade school English when communicating with customers or employees in foreign countries.
- Conduct ourselves as ambassadors of our country and company when in foreign countries.
- Know the laws and customs of the lands we are visiting. Follow them!
- Leverage local knowledge.
- Take care of our employees so they will take care of our company. That's true for all countries.

Chapter Nine

The Greatest Risk
Is
Not Taking One

Bette Nesmith Graham had a problem. A single mom who was sidetracked from artistic aspirations into work as a secretary for the Texas Bank & Trust, she couldn't type—at least not very well. In spite of this handicap, she progressed at the bank and in time was working for the chairman of the board.

One day, Graham watched workers paint the bank windows as part of holiday decorations. When they made a mistake, they just painted over it with white paint. A light went on in Bette's head. Why couldn't she fix typing mistakes in the same way? She mixed up a batch of what she called "Mistake Out" in her kitchen sink, using water-based paint. Always the artist, she drew on those skills now to blend the colors into a perfect match for the paper used at the office. It worked like a charm, and she used her secret weapon against typing errors for five years before co-workers began to catch on and nagged her to share the wealth, so to speak.

Risk is the lubricant that oils the world of opportunity.

The ingredients for her invention changed over time, as Bette was always trying to make it better. There was no money for a chemist, but she patched together a product development team consisting of an office supply worker, a chemistry teacher from the local high school and a friend from a paint store. Soon her son and friends were filling little containers of Mistake Out in her garage. She renamed the product Liquid Paper in 1958, the same year the bank fired her for

147

improper use of their letterhead. In 1961—more than a dozen years after inventing the product—she hired her first employee. By 1968, annual sales had grown to $1 million. Four years later, Bette was selling five million bottles annually from a new corporate headquarters in Dallas. The one-time secretary who risked everything to create a product out of necessity and self-preservation died in 1980, only a few months after selling Liquid Paper to Gillette for $47.5 million.(1)

A Dare Over Dinner

Kate Brosnahan, a Kansas City native, took a different but no less risky path in 1991. Following a dare from her boyfriend during dinner to take things into her own hands, she quit her $14,500 a year job and did just that. Kate was no stranger to risk. She had come to New York with just $7 five years earlier. Since she had worked as an accessories editor, Kate knew about handbags, so handbags it was. The couple's small apartment became design central. Using white paper and scotch tape, Kate designed a half dozen bags and had mockups made. They named the company Kate Spade. (Spade was boyfriend Andy's last name.) The company began selling in 1993.

Kate began attending trade shows, but early orders were disappointing. Eventually, the orders picked up and so did interest in the evolving Kate Spade brand. There was no money for fancy trade show trappings. Instead Kate used quirky flea market finds to display her handbags. It only added to the fresh, stylish appeal of her products. By 1995, this inexperienced business racked up sales of $1.5 million. Kate and Andy plowed all of their savings into the business and took living expenses from Andy's advertising work. In 1996 Kate won a major award from the Council of Fashion Designers of America. From there things started to look up, way up. They added new staff with the experience and industry clout to get them where they wanted to go. In 1999, Kate and Andy cut a deal to sell 56% of the business to Neiman Marcus for $33.6 million. (2)

Fighting To Fly

Southwest Airlines wasn't always everyone's poster child for outrageous customer service and wacky, fun-loving employees who made flying fun and inexpensive. In fact, the story of how Southwest got off the ground is an against-all-odds tale that has done much to shape the attitude and posture of the company to this day. In the early days, the company faced such overwhelming odds against succeeding in the airline business that its employees were locked in one do-or-die struggle after another. Before long, it wasn't just about starting an airline. It was a crusade of epic proportions, and what hung in the balance was Southwest's vision of how a few passionate upstarts could change the world, at least the part that had to do with U.S. air travel. Wielding a mixture of passion, creativity, excitement and sheer guts that would be hard to quantify today, Southwest crafted their mission: To bring enjoyable, affordable air travel to people who never dreamed it could be a reality for them.

Sometimes the magic of a simple, powerfully held idea overcomes every obstacle because its time on the world's stage has come.

Although it is the most famous of startup clichés, Southwest Airline really did began with a vision scratched on a cocktail napkin. Today, that original napkin is represented by a wooden plaque, and it hangs proudly in the airline's Dallas headquarters. In 1966 Rollin King, a San Antonio businessman had an idea for an intrastate airline. King pitched the idea to Herb Kelleher, a lawyer who had done work for a small air service that King owned. Kelleher thought the whole thing was idiotic but was curious enough to begin exploring the brainstorm. And so began an epic five-year battle for the right to fly. During those turbulent years, the only things flying were legal documents—back and forth between lowly Southwest and the airline interests determined to keep the upstart right where it was—on the ground.

In January of 1971, now more than four years since the original concept had first seen the light of day, Southwest hired Lamar Muse as its first CEO. He came aboard when this little airline would have a measly $142 bucks in the bank and past due bills amounting to $80,000. Being a picture of perseverance from day one, Southwest pushed on and finally took off on June 18, 1971, with a number of roundtrips between Dallas and San Antonio and Dallas and Houston. But for Southwest, getting off the ground was only a prelude to performing off the charts on any measure of success you want to name. (3)

Baby Steps To Success

One more. Fast forward to the 90s. Now imagine a new mom with a homemade video she patched together for her daughter Aspen because she couldn't find anything she liked on the market. What she wanted was a baby-friendly introduction to art, literature, music and poetry. What Julie Aigner-Clark created was the Baby Einstein Language Nursery. Mom's gentle, familiar voice was the voiceover talent. Julie and her husband Bill took $10,000 of their savings and made the video, which garnered an instant following among close friends.

Unless somebody, somewhere, somehow steps up and willingly takes a risk, nothing happens.

While the task of building distribution beyond a forgiving network of well-wishing friends was hard work, Baby Einstein made steady progress. After no response from a retailer she thought would be an ideal outlet for her product, Julie Aigner-Clark hopped a plane to New York and prowled the exhibition floor at the 1997 Toy Fair trade show. She was noticed. Her video was taken seriously and within a few months was being test marketed in a handful of stores. Sales were brisk, and the stores wanted more titles. Within a year sales were a respectable $100,000. By the time the Clarks sold Baby Einstein to the Walt Disney Company in 2001 for $25 million, its sales had reached $20 million. (4)

Unless somebody, somewhere, somehow steps up and willingly takes a risk, nothing happens. No one has a job. No one sells a product. No one makes money. Nothing moves or grows or changes. Risk is the lubricant that oils the world of opportunity, keeping it limber, freely moving and ever-ready to take advantage of the next possibility, which of course involves some measure of risk. Why do we take risks? That's an easy one, isn't it? For the potential reward, success, attention or fortune, of course. But what does a risk taker *look* like? What are the characteristics or identifying marks or traits? And why do some risk takers become spectacular winners and others forgotten losers? Well, that's a pretty deep question, and I'm not scholar enough to answer it. I have no expensive research to support my case, mind you, but I do have some opinions, based on the hard lessons of life and business.

Others suffer what's often called analysis paralysis. They study and analyze so completely that it lulls them into inactivity.

First, let's be clear. The obstinate desire to pursue bad ideas breeds unnecessary risks. So the first thing I think a risk taker does is manage his risks, making sure the course he follows has a reasonable chance of success in the first place. Certainly, confidence and persistence are huge parts of a risk taker's makeup. If you have no conviction or strength behind your idea, you'll have no power to persuade others of its worth. I think you also need to be well-informed about the potential outcomes. Perhaps you can't see around the bend, but have you traveled the part of the road you can see and taken heed of what it shows you?

From my experience, risk takers are also given to curiosity, the insatiable yearn to "what if" things and ideas? And, of course, risk takers need to be fundamentally optimistic about life and opportunity. If you're a person for whom the sky is always cloudy, the glass always half empty and the day always a disappointment . . . well, you figure it out.

I used to work with an advertising man who said, "You have to make your own luck." Perhaps he was onto something. It stands to reason that a successful risk taker will be adequately equipped, funded and trained for success. But the spectacular exceptions are usually not in this category. Sometimes the magic of a simple, powerfully held idea will overcome every obstacle because its time on the world's stage has come and nothing can hold it back. In many respects, successful risk taking is the intersection of belief and timing—a perfect storm where the billowing, churning clouds of circumstance, opportunity and inspiration merge into a force of unimaginable power. What else could have driven a Jeff Bezos to pursue the conviction of a successful Amazon when it had amassed billions in debt and zero in profit?

Fear Of Failure

Presumably, those among us who shy away from risks and take as few as possible simply lack the traits of risk takers. Or maybe we have the same characteristics but in the wrong proportions. Haven't you known people who carry "what ifing" way too far? *What if I can't think of a product to follow this one? What if the first product sells but the next one doesn't? What if I can't pay my mother back the money I borrowed from her? What if things get so bad I have to sell my car? What if people laugh when this doesn't work? What if I try this and it doesn't work and I can't find a new job?* Maybe all of this is a smoke screen hiding the golden goose egg in the confidence department.

Having or getting the answers to those questions is really the exact opposite of taking risks. If you knew the answers, it wouldn't be a risk, now would it? Others suffer what's often called analysis paralysis. They study and analyze so completely that it lulls them into inactivity. This is probably another defense mechanism. I know there have been studies conducted among highly successful people, and I know they share some general traits. Personality, circumstances and emotional makeup would seem to have a lot to do with who can stare risk down and become successful and who can't. But I think that nasty little four-letter word *fear* does more harm than any other factor. Call me crazy, but I think fear of failure is the really big kahuna when it comes to risk-averse types looking for ways to avoid laying it all on the line. Failure. How can a handful of innocent letters conjure up such dread and trembling, attach such lasting stigma, and inflict such deep and ugly wounds?

Fundamental optimism—call it persistence if you will—drives the risk taker.

The answer, of course, is that they cannot unless we let them. Remember our discussion of self-awareness and our ability to *inject* choice between stimulus and response? We can choose how we are going to react to a given result. If we choose to believe we have failed, then I guess we'll get what our attitude has ordered up. But if we feel that the result is simply an unacceptable endpoint, then we'll probably go at it again . . . differently. Remember, rejection is what others do to you. Failure is what you do to yourself. Often, when a pessimist doesn't get the result he wants, he concludes failure and quits. Faced with a similar situation, an optimist concludes he had the equation wrong, makes adjustment and tries again. Fundamental optimism—call it persistence if you will—drives the risk taker.

Another Choice, Another Chance

One of the best known examples of persistence is the story of the simple man who would lead many.

- 1816: His family forced out of their home. He had to work to support them.
- 1818: His mother died.
- 1831: Failed in business.
- 1832: Ran for state legislature—lost.
- 1832: Also lost his job. Wanted to go to law school but couldn't get in.
- 1833: Borrowed some money from a friend to begin a business, but by the end of the year he was bankrupt. He spent the next 17 years of his life paying off the debt.
- 1834: Ran for state legislature again—won.
- 1835: Was engaged to be married, but his sweetheart died and his heart was broken.
- 1836: Had a total nervous breakdown and was in bed for six months.
- 1838: Sought to become speaker of the legislature—defeated.
- 1840: Sought to become elector—defeated.
- 1843: Ran for Congress—lost.
- 1846: Ran for Congress again. This time he won, went to Washington and did a good job.
- 1848: Ran for re-election to Congress—lost.
- 1849: Sought the job of land office in his home state—rejected.
- 1854: Ran for Senate of the United States—lost.
- 1856: Sought the Vice-Presidential nomination at his party's national convention—received less than 100 votes.
- 1858: Ran for U. S. Senate again—lost.
- 1860: Abraham Lincoln was elected president of the United States.

Failure: The Path To Success

Both life and business would seem to have an identical lesson: Setbacks are only failures if you don't learn from them. In fact, there is a lot of opinion out there that contends failure is a good thing because it clears the path to eventual success. Where would we be, for example, if Thomas Edison had given up on finding a material for a light bulb's filament after only a few hundred tries instead of sticking with it through the thousands it eventually required? "Sometimes Success Begins at Failure" is the promise of an online article from the Harvard

Business School. It discusses the management of *false negatives* (indicators of failure that turn out to be ultimately false) and uses as an example the fascinating history of Pfizer's Viagra. In the 1980s, the drug company began human testing for compound UK-92,480. Even though it had promising lab results, human trials were disappointing. But recognizing a provocative side effect, scientists were able to turn seeming failure into a spectacular success and a blockbuster product. (5)

If you haven't created an environment where employees feel it's safe to make mistakes, I guarantee they've become entrenched, cautious and tentative.

Others say a startup business's best friend is failure. When a web designer from California launched Dogster.com at the beginning of 2004, failure was the universal prediction, especially after the flamboyant flop of Pets.com. Well, guess what? The site has become a social network for pet owners with hundreds of thousands of human members and even more photos and profiles of pets. What's more, it has attracted advertisers the likes of Disney and Holiday Inn. Did they fail? Of course, but creator Ted Rheingold did what is near and dear to my heart: He failed cheap and fast by launching ideas quickly, analyzing mistakes (by listening to customer feedback) and then fixing them just as fast. (6)

Obviously, we have been talking about the failures of business entities. But fear of failure on a personal level is a cancer that can devour a company's spirit and potential from the inside out. In the end, companies are people and if your people are afraid of failure on the job, it can't help but slow your performance and response. If you haven't created an environment where employees feel it's safe to make mistakes, I guarantee they've become entrenched, cautious and tentative. And they're probably stopping to check policies and procedures every step of the way. They're not practicing self-management, acting like entrepreneurs or maximizing quality or service. They're definitely not thinking like owners.

Nothing is more important than creating that forgiving environment in which making mistakes is okay. Nurturing our precious culture is critical because it is what will sustain us as a "living company," to borrow a phrase from author Arie de Geus. Without constant attention and reinforcement of the profound truths upon which my great grandfather, grandfather and father built Armstrong, all will be lost. I'm trying to do my part, but I know that we are only one generation away from losing what we've invested several lifetimes building.

He failed cheap and fast by launching ideas quickly, analyzing mistakes (by listening to customer feedback) and then fixing them just as fast.

To send the message that it's okay to make mistakes and fail, some companies give awards for right-thinking failures. (7) Others throw parties—which we've done at Armstrong. Southwest Air provides another example of how to handle employees' failure. Its culture encourages employees to be themselves, color outside the lines and try new things. The inevitable outcome will be the occasional failure. But the culture absorbs, heals and transforms to such a degree that employees continue trying . . . and failing once in a while. (8) I think we have the same kind of culture at Armstrong. Read these stories and see what you think.

The Stolen Office

What will you say when this story is over? It begins with Matt Tisch in accounting talking with Janet Babcock in purchasing.

"Janet, how does one get an office around here?"

"Find an empty office and move in. After a while, maybe people will get used to you being there, and then it's yours," she laughs.

"You think so? You think that might work?"

Janet laughs again, "Who knows?"

Later that day, Matt Tisch finds an empty office and moves into it. It doesn't take long before his boss, David Dykstra, Financial Controller, walks into Matt's office.

"Hi, Matt. So how long do you plan on staying here?"

"Well, I've only been here for a few hours. I haven't really thought about it."

"Well, enjoy your new office for the rest of the day," smiles David as he leaves.

The next morning Matt Tisch finds himself at his *old* desk working hard. When he leans back in his chair, he glances across the room and smiles. He sees the name "Matt Tisch" still over the office he almost had.

David's moral: *Behold the turtle, he only makes progress when he sticks his neck out.—James Bryant Conant, President, Harvard University*

Change is the only thing, if big enough, that brings new opportunities. Give me those Armstrongers who are crazy, wacky, daring, adventurous risk takers, and they will bring us revolutionary new products, services and quality improvements. We need more employees like Matt Tisch if we're going to keep Armstrong healthy. Matt's taking an empty office without approval makes an interesting story. The fact that he was asked to leave the office at the end of the day was a failure—but a stylish setback, a failure with flair. I want more people who do things like taking offices without approval. I want more employees who have the spirit, energy and passion for risk taking. To reward Matt for his fearless efforts we gave him the office a few days later.

Through my stories, I have tried to encourage risk takers. Some Armstrongers are beginning to practice risk taking. But many of them are uncomfortable with the changes I'm promoting. Very few of them understand the importance of change and how it will help Armstrong survive. Don't bother stealing an office like Matt. You won't get it. You're just a copy cat. Don't lose sight of the fact that the real risk was in being the *first* to try it and the reward for being fearless – was an office.

Points To Ponder From This Story:

1. **Only big risk will bring revolutionary opportunities.**
2. **Fail with wit, grace and style.**
3. **Risk your job once a day.**

Harold Coop, Inc.

Come with me as we deliver some Armstrong steam traps to Harold Coop, Inc. Armstrong International sub-contracts the painting of our steam traps to Harold Coop, Inc. Harold's company is very small. Actually, he is the only employee. Upon entering his store, I find Harold busy at work painting steam traps. Quietly, I stand back and watch. He takes great pride in making sure that the total surface of the product is covered, and he is careful not to have any runs in the paint. I watch him set the spray gun down and clean it, making sure it is ready for the next job. Carefully, he places each of the products on a conveyer belt which moves them in front of two large fans, which help dry the paint more quickly.

When Harold turned around and saw me, his eyes quickly grew bigger and he jerked his head back. He pulled down his mask (now blue with paint) and smiled.

"Hello. I didn't know you were here. How long have you been waiting?"

"Long enough to watch you take pride in your work. You do a very nice job. Our products look great."

"Thank you . . . so what can I do for you, David?"

"Well, I have been a customer of yours for a long time, as you know, and I couldn't help but notice that your store had a facelift. It looks really good."

"I'm glad you noticed. I spent a lot of time on it. I cleaned all the equipment and repainted it with bright colors to make it more cheerful for our customers."

"You really do love your job don't you?"

"I sure do."

"It shows. I especially like the Armstrong logo painted on your equipment."

David's moral: *If you lose ownership, you lose desire.*

Points To Ponder From This Story:

1. **Keep the spirit of the intrapreneur alive. Harold Coop may be an Armstrong employee using Armstrong equipment, but he thinks like an intrapreneur.**
2. **You can be a valuable brand, just like one of our products. Think Me, Inc.**

Good News, Bad News

This story begins with Henry Nichols of Affiliated Steam placing an order from Eli Lilly, a pharmaceutical company in Indiana. It was November 11, 2005, when Henry called Matt McNamara with quite an "opportunity." Eli Lilly had money to spend BUT it needed delivery by December 23. Matt and Henry discussed what they needed and decided on 29 standard *Low Boy*™ packages.

Matt appeared at the door of the General Manager, Harriett Romig, shortly after his talk with Henry. "Harriet, I have good news and bad news."

"Tell me the good news first," smiled Harriet.

"We have an opportunity to get a 29-package order from Eli Lilly." Harriett's smile grew larger until she noticed that Matt was not smiling.

"Okay, what's the bad news, Matt?"

"They have to be shipped by December 23, and that's only six weeks away."

The first problem Harriett saw was that she didn't have 29 receivers in stock. She immediately called her vendor for receivers. She knew that this vendor's lead times were 12-15 weeks, so she was afraid the situation wasn't very hopeful. After explaining the situation to the vendor and emphasizing that they would lose the order, the vendor agreed to meet the deadline. What a great surprise!

Just as Harriett was about to call Matt, she was informed that the main pipe fitter at Armstrong Fluid Handling, Inc. was scheduled out during that time for knee surgery. Due to project work, all pipe fitters were very busy within sister divisions. Harriett would have to take her chances and go outside, hoping to find somebody in time. Harriett walked over to Matt's office.

"Matt, tell Henry we can do it."

"We have another problem, Harriett. I was just told that seven of the standard packages need to be customized with a special receiver, different piping and new drawings."

"That's okay. We'll still do it." Still no smile from Matt.

"Matt, why the frown?"

"How much more will it cost the customer?"

"Nothing. We'll cover it."

This story ends with 29 *Low Boy*™ packages delivered on time . . . and a smile on Matt's face.

Don't be afraid to go out on a limb for that is where the fruit is. It would have been easy for Harriett to have said "No" to the ship date and "No" to the last-minute customization. Our vendor could have laughed and declined the order. Both fearlessly shouldered a risk. Perhaps they gained strength from one another. "If you can do, I can do it." After all, we are who we hang out with.

Don't be afraid when you have no choice. I find it amazing how many times people do the impossible when they have no choice. And how many fail the possible when there are no problems. Take comfort in tackling the impossible. It has been done before. Be fearless. By the same token, never assume that the obvious is the truth. Matt could have passed on this opportunity and told Henry we couldn't do it. It would have been a reasonable answer to an unreasonable request. But Matt didn't hide behind the safe answer. He became fearless and took a risk.

Points To Ponder From This Story:

1. Don't be afraid to go out on a limb. That's where the fruit is.
2. Don't be afraid when you have no other choice.
3. Never assume the obvious is the truth.

Let's Make A Promise To ...

"Promises we can begin keeping right here, right now." *David Armstrong*

- Use risk to lubricate our opportunities.
- Make something happen, act like an intrapreneur, by taking a risk.
- Try the impossible and remember only big failures create revolutionary products and services.
- Encourage risk taking in our company.
- Celebrate our failures. That will help the item above.
- Don't fall victim to paralysis by a-n-a-l-y-s-i-s.
- Don't fear failure; but embrace it as a confidant who can give us inside information.
- Create an environment where people can fail without punishment.
- Be fearless.

Chapter Ten

Urgency: The Currency of the Future

Life does move in a blur, doesn't it? There's virtual this and virtual that and an e-version of darn near everything nowadays. Technology keeps pushing us, speeding up our world at the same pace it's shrinking it. Inevitably some of us are caught on the fringes and in the folds of this urgency. Too old or scared or tired to keep pace everywhere and in every way, we do the best we can. Many of us have computers of unimaginable potential and versatility on our desks. But do we know their secrets? Are we masters of these mighty midgets? And can we wield their strange and wonderful powers? Heck, I still have problem with our phone system! I would be surprised if I knew and could use 10 percent of my computer's capability.

Want more proof? Remember back when the first ATM machines appeared? Or what about self-service gas pumps? Many of us were uncomfortable with these, and it took years to adapt to the technology. Stand back and watch the confused clot of human frustration that grows at stamp machines and automated kiosks at airports, movie theaters, Home Depot and similar places. The young or youngish are swift and adept. The not-so-very-much-older, aging and elderly are to varying degrees tentative, fumbling and painfully slow—a picture of cautious trial and error every step of the way. Most of us are not willing to operate these self-service contraptions until forced into it. Be honest now. And we've had years to adapt and become comfortable, thanks to the ATM and the self-service gas pump.

In the lawless years of the old American West, gun slingers were fast . . . or dead. The focus was on fast, and if you were, you lived to tell about it and try again another day. If not, somewhere there was a notch on a pistol butt in your memory. My, how things have changed. Or have they? Join the World Fast Draw

Association (WFDA) at www.fastdraw.org and you can still test the speed of your trigger finger against the best in the west—or north, south and east for that matter. Members compete in contests (firing at targets, not each other) around the globe. The organization's Web site says it is ". . . dedicated to governing, preserving and promoting the sport of Fast Draw." Winning draws take only a fraction of a second, so differences of just hundredths of a second can decide matches. Slow may not make you dead anymore, but you're still the loser.

The Future Belongs To The Fast

The evidence surrounds us. Life moves in the fast lane. Hop on a keyboard and access websites from anywhere on planet earth. Board a plane and be continents away in a matter of hours.

Slow may not make you dead anymore, but you're still the loser.

Pick up a phone and have a global presence in as little time as it takes to punch a few buttons on a keypad. And you can do at least two of those things with a compact little device that probably also does duty as a camera, calculator or who knows what else. The rats in the race are still rats, but they're moving faster all the time. And it seems like getting on with life in any significant way depends on getting up to speed and keeping the pedal to the metal.

Not so long ago, one-on-one relationships were a safe haven for a slower pace. After all, the wonderfully mysterious process by which men and women found each other, grew to know and appreciate one another, and finally fell in love and were married was usually a slow and measured undertaking. The very parts of the process so memorable to many of us were pleasant and unhurried. You know—the walks in the park, the deep conversations over long dinners, the endless hours spent together in front of movie screens and concert stages.

Well, no more. Can you hear the wheels of yet another fond memory come screeching to a halt? TA DA! It's time for speed dating, baby! Yep. Seems like a lot of singles today are just too busy to meet people. If you don't opt for the bar scene and are not keen on dating co-workers, so the story goes, speed dating may be just what Cupid ordered. According to wikipedia.org, the idea is to facilitate meeting a large number of new people quickly. The idea is credited to Rabbi Yaacov Deyo of Aish who came up with it as a way of helping Jewish singles to meet and marry. The first official "event" was in 1998 at a café in Beverly Hills, CA.

It goes something like this. After paying a fee to take part in one of these events, singles meet a number of people in a quick succession of "dates" (conversations) lasting only a few minutes each. At whatever the interval happens to be (usually no more than 10 minutes), a bell or signal sounds and everyone rotates to the next "date." At the end, attendees pass on to organizers the names of the party or parties with whom they want to share contact information. When a match occurs, information is passed to both parties. Exchanging contact information during the dating portion is prohibited.

With 8minuteDating, one of the leaders in the field, you get eight one-on-one sessions lasting eight minutes each. In early 2006 the organization held a pre-Valentine's Day event in 33 states and 93 cities and towns across the U.S. The goal is to provide a fast, fun, safe and comfortable way to meet people in-person and establish dating, friendship or business connections. Founded in 2001, 8minuteDating has held more than 4,000 events across the country. (1)

Urgency is about how you think. I really believe that only the quick will survive.

At their very heart, the problems of the American automobile industry, to take a popular example, revolve around the loss of urgency. Just doing things fast is not enough. Having a sense, having a culture, focused on urgency means there is an understanding of *why* things need to be done quickly, *what* will happen when you do, and *who* will ultimately benefit.

Urgency is a way of life, a strategy for success. I hope every Armstrong employee understands the importance of speed – and takes action. Urgency is attitude. The faster things get, the faster we want them. The computer program that takes a few seconds to load seems exasperatingly slow. I know I'm guilty. I'm spoiled. I want it NOW. I recently did a little experiment that drilled several things home to me. The first was the enormity of the Internet as an information resource. The second was the almost magical ability of search engines to locate information. And third? That would be my growing dependence on the first two—and it happened almost without my recognition. Fifteen years ago the Internet did not exist, at least in any mainstream way. Today, it dictates how and at what pace we live our lives.

Our Need For Speed

I have a need for speed, is the anthem of the dot.com era. And much of speed in the world of commerce today comes from the capacity of the Internet to make it so. As part of the research for this project, I wanted to play with Internet search engines, specifically Google. My wife has always been partial to the Lincoln Navigator we once owned. So this became the first subject of my little test. I typed it in. In 0.11 seconds, I was presented with the first 10 of 2,180,000 entries. More than two million in less than half a second! How is this possible? How do they do it? Warming to my task, I cast about for another search subject. I know, the steam trap. After all, that has been Armstrong's primary product for more than a century. Into the little search box goes "steam traps." Enter. Incredible! 1,920,000 in 0.17 seconds. Okay, this is fun.

But let's narrow it down and be specific. So this time I typed in "Armstrong inverted bucket steam traps." Enter. Would you believe 13,900 in 0.15 seconds? Next, I tried "Armstrong International, Stuart, FL." In just 0.15 seconds I had 760,000 references. Such power and potential completely baffle and amaze me— especially when I reflect on the fact that the phenomenon that became Google.com was first patched together by two twenty-something whiz kids in their dorm room.

The faster things get, the faster we want them.

The whiz kids' names were Larry Page and Sergey Brin. They met in 1995 when they were both PhD candidates at Stanford. Page was from the University of Michigan and 24 years old. Sergey was 23, and he was one of a group assigned to show Page around campus. Initially, things did not go well, and the two argued about everything. But by the beginning of 1996 the duo was collaborating on a search engine project they called BackRub because of its ability to leverage the "back links" pointing to web sites. The results were good, and BackRub began to attract attention but no buyers. So they decided to go into business themselves, transforming Page's dorm room into their first data center patched together with parts from cheap PCs and a few thousand dollars from their maxed-out credit cards.

In 1998 they moved to a garage in Menlo Park, CA. By this time they had hired four employees and begun to scrape together funds from friends, family and hopeful investors. One of the latter was Andy Bechtolsheim, a founder of Sun Microsystems. After a brief demo in the garage, Bechtolsheim, who was pressed for time due to a previous commitment, wrote a check for $100,000 on the spot. That was the good news. The bad was that he made it out to Google, Inc. which did not yet exist as a legal entity. So they stowed the check in a desk drawer until they could make arrangements to set the entity up and continue fundraising. When it was all said and done, they had nearly $1 million in seed money. By the summer of 1999 they secured additional funding from venture capitalists to the tune of $25 million (which is now worth some $4 billion). Before long, the company was responding to 10,000 search requests per day. By the end of 2000, the number was 60 million each day. By 2005, search requests per day had grown to—are you ready for this?—200 million per day. (2)

Urgency will always be in demand. It is the currency of the future.

From the very beginning, Larry Page and Sergey Brin zeroed in with fanatical focus on just one goal—search efficiency. How to do it? Subordinate everything else to speed and accuracy. To this day, Google's home page is the very picture of simplicity. As for that name? A note on a page of the company's Web site entitled "Corporate Information" says it is a play on the word "googol." Milton Sirotta, a relative of American mathematician Edward Kasner coined it and later made it more popular through *Mathematics and the Imagination* by Kasner and James Newman. It stands for the number 1 followed by 100 zeros. The use of the term reflects Google's mission: To organize the seemingly infinite quantity of information on the Web. (3)

Speed Kills Competition

Speed. A sense of urgency about time, place, actions and priorities. Both foreshadow a practical working knowledge of and the ability to leverage a profound truth of life: *Opportunity waits for no man*. Bill Gates knew about urgency and understood the benefits of harnessing it. From the beginning, Gates could anticipate market needs and make out the shape of opportunity when it was still a speck on the horizon. In 1975 a friend (Paul Allen) showed Bill a feature in *Mechanix Illustrated* about the Altair 8800, the world's first personal computer.

Although it was clunky by modern standards, its parts cost less than $400. While many geeks were probably salivating about getting access to the device, Allen and Gates pondered a different question: *How will Altair get the software they'll need to run this thing?* Within a month they had set out to find the answer. Bill Gates dropped out of Harvard and moved with Paul Allen to Albuquerque, New Mexico, where the 8800 was made. They set up shop literally across the street from Altair as Micro-Soft. Following software successes with Altair, they attracted the attention of Commodore, RadioShack, Texas Instruments and NCR.

By 1980 IBM was knocking on Microsoft's door. (The hyphen was dropped earlier.)

Gates hired the programmer who had developed what was to become the MS-DOS operating system, did some quick fixes and licensed it to IBM. IBM made two key decisions that sealed Microsoft's fortune. One was to license software rather than develop its own. The second was to allow other manufacturers to license its PC designs, which created a huge market of IBM clones—all needing Microsoft software to do anything. When Apple introduced the Macintosh with its groundbreaking point-and-click interface, a renewed sense of urgency surged through Bill Gates. His response was Windows. While early versions did not measure up to Apple, it has steadily grown into the world standard. When Microsoft introduced Windows 95 in 1995, it sold 11 million copies in the first five minutes. At this very moment, about nine of every 10 personal computers in the entire world run some variation of Microsoft Windows and probably several other Microsoft programs as well.

At Armstrong, there is never a better time for action than now.

Speed kills competition. Michael Dell understood this as well as Bill Gates. When Dell was just 18, he wondered why someone couldn't simply buy the parts that make up a computer, put them together and sell the computer directly to the consumer through the mail. He started doing just that from his University of Texas dorm room. Six years later he employed 1,600 and had an estimated net worth of $100 million. The motto that sustained his company and made him at 31 the youngest CEO to ever join the elite company of the *Fortune* 500 is simple enough: *Celebrate for a nanosecond. Then move on.* It is interesting to note that the problems Dell's business has experienced recently are blamed by more than one business commentator on the company's loss of urgency.

Urgency Is My Job

When I became CEO of Armstrong International, I thought very deliberately about what I wanted my legacy to be. What do I want to be known for in the years ahead? What do I want my reputation to be? I came up with four non-negotiable items—core values/ethics/personal and corporate integrity, enjoyable experiences, urgency, and storytelling as a communication/management style. Urgency will always be in demand. It is the currency of the future. Everyone around here knows that you can never be quick enough to make me happy. I am impatient. It's never quick enough, and I always talk about urgency. My FIRST questions normally center on timetables, due dates . . . you know, blinding speed.

Urgency has become my reputation, and I have worked hard to establish it. I have set out to create a reputation for urgency because I think emphasizing it is a way to increase initiative. If I'm always sending signals about the need to find ways to do things with greater urgency, I believe people will begin to get more inventive about how to accomplish what I want. They will believe in my cause and, more importantly, live it every day—ooops, I mean every second. How's that for urgency? Remember, you can be just one word away from your reputation being extinct.

And yes, pursuing urgency will inevitably lead to more mistakes and failed attempts. That's okay. As long as we don't sacrifice quality or safety in the name of urgency, I will ALWAYS encourage employees to be the swiftest. Of all my seven Ss (Swiftest, Simplest, Smallest, Spirit of Intrapreneurship, Surprise, Storytelling and Smiles) it is the most important. The other six support or describe how it is to be delivered. At Armstrong, there is never a better time for action than now. And what you may lose by waiting is opportunity. A few stories will illustrate what I mean.

Excuse Me!

*I*t was late autumn when we found ourselves at Everlasting Valve in South Plainfield, New Jersey. Shortly after arriving, I was in the machine shop talking to John Caulfield, Machine Operator. We were talking about the production bonus and how good it was that month. We couldn't have been talking more than 10 minutes when John Hrin walked down an aisle 30 feet away. John looked over to John Caulfield and shouted, "John, a customer needs his product. I need you back here." He pointed down the aisle to his machine and continued walking in that direction.

"I guess I better go help him. I was supposed to do that a few minutes ago."

I smiled and said, "Sure. I'll talk to you later."

I continued my tour. Later, I found myself at John Hrin's machine. John was working on a large stainless steel valve on his machine.

"John, you made my day," I said as I put my hand on his shoulder.

"I did?"

"Yes, you did. When you interrupted John Caulfield and me, you showed you weren't afraid to interrupt management in order to service our customers. There aren't many employees out there who would have interrupted us. The customer comes first, and you understand that."

"Well, I knew you wouldn't mind, David. This order has to ship today." He pointed to the stainless steel valve. "And I needed John's help."

"You were right. Feel free to interrupt me anytime to service our customers."

David's moral: *Everyone's first job is swiftly serving the customer.*

This is a tough one for me. I see it so simply and clearly, and I am at a loss as to why others can't as well. People just don't get it. In fact, I've come to believe that the surest way to make enemies is to ask someone to do something faster. The common response is to attempt to slow me down, to ask for more time. The reasons are many and usually include the fear of poor quality, the desire for more information and the fear of failure. While employees may say they understand and believe in urgency, their actions tell a different story. They don't live it and model it in how they behave, at least not every day. They're looking for ways to escape the intensity of urgency, not for a means of embracing it.

John Hrin and John Caulfield understand that the customer comes first. How many employees do you have who are not afraid to excuse themselves from talking to a high-level manager or the owner of the company? John Caulfield was not afraid to excuse himself, and John Hrin was not afraid to interrupt my conversation. The order must ship on time as promised. Both men understand and live urgency in the servicing of our customers. Both of them are devoted to making things faster, and they made my day because of it. See if you can identify with the sense of urgency in the next story.

Points To Ponder From This Story:

1. The only thing we have to fear is "fear of urgency."
2. *If* you want to make enemies, try to speed something up.

Hear Etta Page, See Grant Run

𝒯his story begins each day in the parking lot between Plant 1 and Plant 3 of Armstrong International, Inc. in Three Rivers, MI. Throughout the day, you will find Armstrongers walking between the plants checking on orders, moving parts, repairing machines, etc. It's not a short walk. Probably 500 feet of parking lot separate the two plants. (To understand why this is so, read "Our Promise to Fred Kemp" in my book, *Managing By Storying Around*, or in this book.)

A lot of times people ride our Armstrong "people movers" (golf carts) to save time. But there are still those who like the exercise and walk across the parking lot to the next plant. Grant Kain is one of these Armstrongers. Grant has a nice steady walking pace—not too fast and not too slow. But when he hears the loudspeakers blast out: **Grant Kain, would you please dial 322**, he begins to run to the nearest phone.

David's moral: *Know the difference between moving fast and having a sense of urgency.*

Although there is no string attaching Etta Griffin (Grant's secretary) to Grant, you would think there was by how easily she can jerk him into action. Her public address page is just like pulling a string and turning Grant on, so to speak.

When I re-read this story, I tend to think of alternative morals. One that springs to mind is: "When leaders run, followers should sprint." Okay, so it's not poetic, but you get the idea. One of the primary responsibilities of a leader is to keep urgency alive and well, and believe me, it's a big job. You can talk about it all day long, but people still love to procrastinate. When Armstrongers feel uncomfortable with their slow pace while around their leaders, I think it's time for their leaders to notch it up a bit. Kick it into a higher gear. People *notice* urgency, and it is a catalyst for action. Ed Kirchner told me this story. He began with, "Hear Etta Page, See Grant Run." I told Ed I didn't believe him, but Stu Warner, who heard Ed tell me this story, confirmed it. So, you see, people do notice urgency.

Urgency (time) is the currency of the future. Time will be more valuable than quality. It will be more important than innovation. It will be more precious than service, and it will become the key to success in any business. No one has enough time. Help your customers save it, and they will pay you handsomely for it. The next story is an ideal example of that fact.

Points To Ponder From This Story:

1. A prime responsibility of a leader is to keep urgency alive.
2. Time is the currency of the future.
3. Visibly practice urgency for all to see – like running to a phone.

Armstrong's Demo Van

*D*on Hail, President of Hughes Machinery, tells a wonderful story about service. The Riverside Seat Company manufactures automobile seats on a just-in-time contract for the General Motors' Fairfax Assembly Plant in Kansas City, Kansas. The last step of the manufacturing process is to stretch and fluff the cloth seats by steaming them. Riverside uses a small steam boiler. On a Thursday their steam system went down due to corrosion and scaling problems. Riverside had to tell General Motors that they could not steam the seats coming off their assembly line. The choices for GM were: 1) shut down the line or 2) accept wrinkled seats to be steamed in the cars later. General Motors opted for the latter to avoid shutting down the line, but they were then faced with the dilemma of having some 200 cars not ready for shipment. If they had to hold the cars over until the end of the month, they had to be carried on the books for another month.

Therefore on Thursday evening, May 26, Riverside and General Motors were looking for a portable boiler system. During a conference call, they realized that a small boiler on wheels had just pulled into the parking lot—the Armstrong Demo Van! We had to line up our people to deliver the van, supervise the contractor on piping the van into a manifold for the steamers and start up and operate the boiler. About an hour after the first call, our serviceman, Bill McIntosh, and Alan Schneider, our Inside Sales Engineer, went to Riverside. By 9:00 p.m., everything was ready. The next morning, Jim Wonderly, Sales Engineer, reported at 5:00 a.m. By 2:30 p.m. all 200 seats were steam ironed and ready for delivery. Jim shut down and secured the van and headed back to Hughes Machinery.

David's Moral: *Urgency eliminates obstacles and solves problems.*

Each Armstrong division has a different strategy for business success. Some choose innovation. Others pick service or quality. No matter what the strategy, I always want them to proceed with urgency. Why? Because speed kills competition. Be the first with a new product, have the fastest delivery or be the first to introduce a quality breakthrough. "Make urgency how you implement your plan," I always tell them. While speed is no secret to our customers because they see us practice it every day, it is one of the secrets of our success. It's not really a secret because any company can do likewise, but few will commit to the effort. The secret lies in living urgency, breathing speed, thinking fast and acting quickly.

And the best of all this good news? *You can charge more for speed.* The newest products usually have the highest prices and produce higher profits. Quicker service demands a higher price. Obviously, when the quality is higher, so is the price.

Urgency is the ultimate weapon in business. Without urgency, neither quality, service nor innovation will succeed as a business strategy. Even those who use low prices as their marketing weapon will fail if they are not the first in the market with the lowest prices.

Points To Ponder From This Story:

1. **Speed kills competition.**
2. **Speed is Armstrong's secret.**
3. **Speed is no enemy to profits.**
4. **Urgency is the ultimate weapon because you can apply it to any business strategy.**

Waxing Floors

*H*e stood six feet, six inches tall, which made the job of waxing the shop floors of Computrol in Boise, Idaho, that much more difficult. Leaning over the buffing machine from his height soon made his back ache. This should have come as no surprise to Charlie Scott. After all, he was 40 years old, not a young man. It also didn't help that this was not his normal job at Computrol. Charlie knew that a large customer, an original equipment manufacturer (OEM), was coming to visit the factory. For weeks, management had tried to schedule stripping the floors clean and waxing them with a special wax that prevents static electricity. Static electricity causes scrap when assembling electronic products. Computrol wanted to make a good impression on the customer so they scheduled some people from a temp agency to wax the floors. Unfortunately, the day they were to arrive, two did not show. There was no time left. The floors had to be waxed. Charlie's regular job would have to wait. He decided to help scrub the floors that morning. While he worked, Charlie listened to the temporary employee working beside him.

"Boy, this job stinks. I really hate this."

"Good morning, Charlie," interrupted an employee as she walked by.

The temp continued, "The money is poor, but the people are really nice and friendly. I hope the management here appreciates these people, but they probably don't. Computrol is probably just like any other company, and the management doesn't care about its people. Or they say they do, but they don't show it."

Charlie kept scrubbing the floor as he listened. Another employee passed by. "Good morning, Charlie."

"So, Charlie, what do you do here at Computrol?" The temp asks.

Charlie looked up with a smile on his face. "I'm the President of Computrol, but today I'm cleaning the floors with you."

The temporary person was both shocked and embarrassed. "So that's why everybody knows you."

David's moral: *The speed of the leader determines the speed of the employees.*

Ronald Reagan once observed, "I'm a prisoner of my schedule again." So was Charlie Scott . . . but he escaped. One might think that as President of Computrol,

Charlie had more important things to do than scrub floors. Not true! Charlie had a culture of urgency to promote. If the President of the company has time to clean floors, then no one can use the excuse, "I don't have time. My schedule is too full." (See also "The Throne" in *Managing By Storying Around*.)

As a leader, take every opportunity that comes your way to promote urgency. Your actions, even if little, get noticed. I believe many *small* actions of urgency are more effective motivation than a few *big* actions of urgency. But remember, practicing urgency is not just for leaders—it's for everybody. Read the next story to see what I mean.

Points To Ponder From This Story:

1. As a leader, take every opportunity to promote urgency.
2. Promoting urgency is not just for leaders—it's for everybody.

The Day I Paid $248,000 to Play Golf

Come with me to the Sailfish Point Golf Course in sunny Florida. As I waited to tee off on the first hole, I thought to myself, "If my office needs me, they know I have my mobile phone." But the phone never rang all day.

When I returned to the office, I found a phone message on my desk: "Please call Jerry Gilchrist." As I dialed the number, I thought to myself, "Good. I'm glad somebody needs me."

"Hi, Jerry. I'm returning your call."

"Hi, David. I just bought two Computer Numeric Controlled (CNC) machines made by Wassino for $248,000."

I paused on the phone. "Jerry, what's the delivery time on these machines?"

"They're available within the week."

"Where are you going to find room to put them?"

"We thought about scrapping or selling one of the single spindle machines and putting the two new machines around the Okuma CNC. That way, one man can run three machines at once.

"Will these machines run unmanned?"

"No, but we will get the machines next week which will help us with our current delivery problems. We can also use these machines on our new valve line."

"I remember last week we were talking about looking at used machines. Are these the used machines?"

"Yes. The reason we had to move so quickly to buy them was because another party was interested. Don Ely called me from the seller location for a quick decision. He's checked the tolerances, maintenance and hours operated on the CNCs. They have only been used six months. The machines look to be in great condition. Before I gave final approval to buy the machines, I talked to Steve Gibson and Ron Schlesch. With their positive comments and with the recommendation of Don Ely, I decided to buy the machines—even though it was more than 12 times my spending authority."

"Jerry, I think you made a good decision."

David's moral: *Never put off 'til tomorrow what should be done today.*

You never know when an urgent decision must be made. If a key decision maker is not available, it shouldn't matter if you have created an environment in your company where people feel comfortable, empowered and supported. Jerry had a spending limit of $20,000, but he spent $248,000. He checked with other responsible parties before making his decision, but he was prepared to be held personally accountable. He felt comfortable spending more than 12 times his authorized limit because he had faith in the Armstrong way of doing things. Once again, mutual trust ruled the day.

Points To Ponder From This Story:

1. **You never know when an urgent decision must be made. So create an environment where your leaders and employees will take action without fear.**
2. **Rules are meant to be broken—given the right circumstances.**
3. **The questions you ask will determine the attitude of your people. I did not challenge Jerry as to why he took action, but asked questions of support and interest.**

Let's Make A Promise To ...

"Promises we can begin keeping right here, right now." *David Armstrong*

- Believe: The future belongs to the Swiftest. Not the swift.
- Remember that speed is action, but urgency is attitude.
- Believe: Only the quick will survive.
- Make urgency a way of life, a strategy for success.
- Always demand and deliver urgency. It is the currency of the future.
- Remember that opportunity waits for no one.
- Remember that speed kills competition.
- Remember that speed is the most important element of strategy.
- Make urgency our job.
- Recognize and accept our responsibility to keep urgency alive and well.
- Make speed profit's best friend.

David Armstrong

Chapter Eleven

Adrift in a World of Change

Change is constant. Change is inevitable. Change is both good and bad.

Yet the very idea of change mystifies me. Oh, I know what it is. I just don't claim to understand it. I think of it as something akin to weather. Think about it. Weather surrounds us all the time. It is always moving, shifting. We can't control it. We can't really predict it even though we have some broad understanding of its general trends and patterns. We can't really escape it. Wherever we go on the planet, we will find it in one form or another. It is infinitely variable, immensely interesting and often frightening in its extremes.

If you add to the things going on in the *atmosphere* surrounding the earth (weather), the seismic, geological and geothermal changes impacting the earth itself, then you have a real party. One of the most extraordinary things about these natural changes is the immense continuum over which they can occur. In their extreme, they can affect vast areas of the earth and its peoples. Or they can be very, very specific—devastating one small area or group of people while the rest of the world has no knowledge of it.

A tornado bears down on a Kansas town in the middle of the night, destroying homes and businesses. By daylight the awful truth is apparent. Fourteen dead and millions in damage. The town's only doctor is dead. The pastor of the Methodist Church loses his wife. Suddenly families are ripped apart, missing one or both parents. In a space of 90 seconds, the forces of change have altered life in this small town for all time. For the inhabitants, nothing is bigger or more important than what's just happened, understandably so, and it will take them years to recover. Their lives will move in different directions from this point, permanently sidetracked onto a new course by a seemingly random twist.

God does not make bad things happen, but in His unlimited power, He can use bad things for good purposes.

However, in Belgium a family takes a meal on their patio in the pleasant coolness. They are expecting the eldest daughter to visit today with their first grandchild. It is a happy day. Life is good. On the shores of Lake Victoria in Africa, a three-year old boy plays in the mud with his sister. They don't even know there is a Kansas. Even in a different part of America, in the state of Maine, what is the most important thing in the world on this day in that Kansas community gets a five-second mention in the local Maine evening news. Nothing more.

Changes Felt 'Round The World

Other events are so large and significant that they affect huge areas and massive numbers of people. For some it is a direct impact. For many, many others it is an indirect connection, rippled out from the center of the change. One of these occurred beneath the waves of the Indian Ocean on December 26, 2004, when a 9.0 earthquake off the coast of Sumatra spawned an immense tsunami. When the massive wave made landfall, it killed hundreds of thousands and did billions in damage. India, Indonesia, Malaysia, the Maldives, Myanmar, Somalia, Sri Lanka and Thailand all suffered major damage and casualties. Bangladesh, Kenya, Seychelles, South Africa, Tanzania and Yemen recorded some casualties and less serious damage. A handful of other nations suffered damage but no casualties. The following is a list of nations that reported citizens dead or missing as a result of the tsunami.

- Argentina
- Australia
- Austria
- Belgium
- Brazil
- Canada
- Chile
- China
- Colombia
- Croatia
- Czech Republic
- Denmark
- Estonia
- Finland
- France
- Germany
- Greece
- Hong Kong

- Ireland
- Israel
- Italy
- Japan
- Luxembourg
- Mexico
- Netherlands
- New Zealand
- Norway
- Philippines
- Poland
- Portugal
- Republic of China

- Russia
- Singapore
- South Africa
- South Korea
- Spain
- Sweden
- Switzerland
- Turkey
- Ukraine
- United Kingdom
- United States
- Vietnam (1)

Powerlessness in the face of change is a source of great concern, fear and frustration for many. Why bad things happen to good people is a topic of unending debate, intensified by each new catastrophe claiming innocent lives. Many are quick to point to such events as proof that there really is no God. For if a truly loving God really existed, He wouldn't allow such things to happen they argue. Christians, of course, believe otherwise. Bad things happen in the world because mankind disobeyed God and misused the gift of free will. God gave man the ability to choose, and we chose wrong. As a result, sin entered the world. Bad things happen. God does not make bad things happen, but in His unlimited power; He can use bad things for good purposes. That is the essence of the comfort that faith brings to those who believe.

Jeremiah 29:11 says, *"For I know the plans I have for you"*, declares the Lord, *"plans to prosper you and not to harm you, plans to give you hope and a future." (NIV)* Or listen to Romans 8:28 which promises, *And we know that in all things God works for the good of those who love him, who have been called according to his purpose.* The support that comes from faith in Bible verses like these is especially important when we consider change of a different sort—the change wrought by human hands.

There are many things outside my control that unleash change on Armstrong. That's when attitude comes into play.

When a group of foreign thugs decided they wanted to change the world for all time by turning airliners into weapons, we were aghast at the evil of which man is capable. The events of 9/11 are another extraordinary example of the power and sweep of change, this time created by man. While relatively few of the world's citizens were in harm's way, look at how the effects of what occurred that day ricocheted around the globe and multiplied their effects across countless lives.

- **115** Nations who had citizens killed.
- **1,609** Individuals who lost a spouse or partner.
- **3,051** Estimate of children who lost a parent.
- **20** Percentage of our people who knew someone injured or killed.
- **146,100** Number of jobs lost in New York City.
- **684** Number of points lost by the Dow Jones Industrial Average when the market reopened.
- **$105 billion** Economic loss to New York in the month following.
- **$40.2 billion** Estimated value of 9/11-related insurance paid worldwide.
- **1.2 million** American citizens who switched 2001 holiday travel from plane to car or train.(2)

Your Attitude Is All You Can Control

Yes, change is a paradox for me. On one hand, I never feel as small and insignificant as when I reflect on the forces of change—both natural and human-initiated—that swirl in and around the world. What happens in the world can end up affecting me in the same way it impacts untold millions of others. And it does so completely out of my reach. I have no opportunity or capacity to alter, temper or divert it. Within the world of Armstrong International, however, my odds improve dramatically. As CEO, I have the capacity to engineer change and to steer it to the way of my liking. I can temper it, soften it or change its direction. I don't have absolute power in this regard, of course, but what I'm saying is that, at least within this part of my existence, I have some measure of control over the changes that our people initiate. The same is true of the leaders in any company.

Still, there are many things outside my control that unleash change on Armstrong. That's when attitude comes into play. We've talked about this in other chapters. Changes are results, and we have some control over how we are going to respond to those results (changes). I like to say it's the difference between herding life or being stampeded by it. If a negative change occurs as a result of a bad work habit or poor judgment, that's a situation we can expect to improve. We just need to retrace our steps, gain a clear view of how we arrived, and then change the chain of events leading up to the result.

Sometimes I find that there are things my father and his management team did in the past that were right in the past but wrong today. So I have to make a change. My change is not an implication that my father made a mistake because change occurs over time, and what was right in the past may be wrong today. I have found that many leaders are concerned about making a change to their boss's past decisions in fear that he/she may be upset. This fear prevents necessary evolutionary change. Remember, your leader made changes to his boss's decisions and so can you.

Other changes happen to Armstrong just as they do to other companies. Again, the trick is in the responding. A supplier ups his price for key components in one our products. A municipality, state or foreign country in which we operate passes new laws that impact our business. One of the most important members of my Executive Committee resigns due to a family or health crisis. A competitor blindsides us with a remarkably good product innovation. In a surprise move, three key competitors merge into one global powerhouse. For reasons no one can figure out there is a shortage of stainless steel (or fill in the blank); the price skyrockets. An offshore supplier begins to undercut us seriously on an entire line of products. The workers building a new plant for us go on strike. And on it goes.

Remember, too, that I'm a guy who likes to keep the pot stirred. In fact, I don't mind keeping my people a little off balance. As Doug Bloss, our Vice President, once said, "Get used to being uncomfortable." It helps prepare them for dealing with unexpected circumstances. I don't want them complacent. I think there's something wrong if they can predict exactly how their day will go, day after day. What I'm saying is that—in addition to the changes that happen to us as individuals and as a corporate entity—I am in the business of deliberately creating positive change. Our people can't create solutions that are the swiftest, simplest and smallest if they are stuck in a rut. They can't wield a spirit of intrapreneurship, use storytelling with a smile and a surprise if they think the way to do something is exactly the way we did it yesterday. Oh, don't get me wrong! There are obviously manufacturing protocols, standard procedures and expected patterns of behavior.

Of course. But no two days are exactly alike. So why should our responses to them be? In fact, on many occasions we are confronted with a situation (opportunity) for which we have no precedent or procedure. They won't find the answer in a rule book or policy manual. (But they might find a hint among our stories.) Where they will eventually discover how to respond, of course, is within their own makeup, experience and collaboration with co-workers. They will find it within the spirit and tradition of Armstrong.

I don't mind keeping my people a little off balance. It helps prepare them for dealing with unexpected circumstances.

Unless our people have had practice at thinking on their feet and looking for solutions in all the unexpected places, they'll be lost. And if they're lost, do you think we'll be able to send the customer away with a smile on her face and an enjoyable experience tucked among her lasting impressions? Me neither.

Remember, Make It Simple

When it comes to dealing with change, I think one of my most important contributions as a leader is actually two-fold. The first part has to do with creating an environment that *promotes* change. The second is modeling a plan for *managing* it. I also believe I must provide an atmosphere that welcomes change and risk taking. And finally, in the midst of change, we must hold fast to the things that never change—our core values. Let's just be straight about the basics. Change is constant. Change is inevitable. Change is not always bad. In fact, since we've focused a good deal on unhappy examples, let's do a little to balance the equation.

Most of the impressions of the 1950s are of a safe, stable and innocent decade. The World War was over, the economy stable and Americans were enjoying new homes in the suburbs. Life was good. But the poliomyelitis virus lurked in the shadows. Entering its victims through the mouth, the virus then multiplied in the intestines and invaded the nervous system. In the 1950s, the prognosis for those infected was grim: One of every 200 infections would lead to paralysis, and up to 10 percent of those would die due to failure of essential breathing muscles. In 1952 there were more than 57,500 polio cases in America. In 1954 polio killed more than 1,300 (mostly children) and crippled some 18,000 more.

On April 12, 1955, news spread that Dr. Jonas Salk had developed a successful vaccine against polio. Once the vaccine became widely available, polio cases in the United States fell by 85-90 percent. In 1961, the world received a simple oral vaccine, thanks to Dr. Albert Sabin. Shortly after the turn of the century, large sections of the world were certified to be polio-free. Total worldwide incidence of polio had fallen to about 1,250 in 2004. (3)

It was 1975… the AMC Gremlin automobile was posting a good year, Captain Beefheart and the Magical Band was a hot group and the Altair 8800, the world's first personal computer, was selling for $421 or two hundred bucks higher if you wanted it to come fully assembled. The name was supplied by the 12-year old daughter of one of the developers after watching an episode of *Star Trek*. (4) From the debut in 1975, personal computers were selling at a clip of several hundred thousand per year through the late 70s. The rate jumped to 1.6 million with the unveiling of IBM's PC in 1981. Growth in shipments continued at double-digit rates through the turn of the century. Only in 1985 and 2001 did shipments decline. The billionth computer is estimated to have shipped in early 2002. (5)

My plan for managing change is as simple as remembering a few fundamentals.

I want Armstrong employees to be change gourmets. Say what? Gourmet chefs are creative, given to experimenting, exploring and discovering the possibilities of new combinations. The goal is to create exciting new sensations from variations in or unique alliances of known ingredients. Change, in this case, is not only good, it can taste good, too. A cook follows a set recipe time after time, but a gourmet lives to experiment.

Two of the most important things I can do for my company is nurture an environment that relishes change and then prove every day that I will manage change with integrity, honesty and adherence to what we believe as a company. I understand that people worry and that when emotion gains the upper hand over rationality, they forget what they've always known. Let's face it. Fears about changes affecting employment dwarf all others (except for the big, life-altering events) for most people. J. K. Rowling is no match for an active imagination set loose by rumors of impending change at work. You know it as well as I do.

Unfortunately, a lot of change is about making things different instead of better. While it may seem elementary, my plan for managing change is as simple as remembering a few fundamentals. The first is to start with the prize in mind. What are we shooting for? Why are we undertaking this change? If it's not about a new product, service, improving our quality, our safety or our relationships with our people and our customers so they have many enjoyable experiences, we're wasting our time. If it is about one of these, then the next question is, Can we accomplish it in line with our core values, mission and vision? And then, of course, making the change needs to apply the seven S strategies. I don't mean to sound as if running a multi-million dollar corporation is simplistic, but it really does come down to a few fundamental truths which we protect at all costs and apply with all passion. But see for yourself...

"Shut Up and Eat Your M&Ms"

My problem was simple: How was I going to get people to accept new ideas? Change is always threatening. When things change, people don't know where they stand. It's not surprising, then, that people invariably resist change. We all know that. Yet we need to keep adapting to an ever-changing marketplace. What do you do? My solution was to hand out M&Ms.

It all started when I learned about a heat-sensitive paint that changes color with temperature. I began to wonder if there was a way we could use it on any of our products. I knew the initial reaction of our senior engineers and salespeople would be: "It's too gimmicky."

"We sell engineered products."

"Our current paint is good enough."

"Why would we want to fool around with something like that?"

To make sure I didn't hear those kinds of things, I told everyone at the meeting that we were there to discuss new ideas, and then I handed everyone an M&M. "You are allowed one negative comment during the meeting," I said. "Once you make that comment, you must eat your M&M. If you don't have an M&M in front of you, you can't say anything negative."

It was great! Instead of being threatened by new ideas, people supported them. Anything negative was instantly met with a joking "Shut Up and Eat Your M&M."

We even got a new product idea out of it—steam traps that change color when they stop working. I'm buying more M&Ms.

David's moral: *Minds are like parachutes. They only function when open.*
M&M is a registered trademark of Mars, Incorporated.

We talk a lot about being creative at Armstrong. I want people to bend the rules, get out of their comfort zones and look for new and unexpected ways to solve problems. But just talking about it won't cut it. If you want people to be creative, *you* have to be creative. Maybe this story will move you beyond the talking stage.

Saying to people, "Okay, now be creative," is like saying, "Okay, we're going to have fun now." Both creativity and fun grow naturally out of the situation and the peculiar chemistry of people, place and context. You just can't engineer it in any predictable fashion. Direct orders from the boss to "change your behavior" rarely work. At least not for long. Why? Because it's contrary to the natural order. If I had said, "From this day forward, you can only make constructive comments at meetings," I doubt that things would have changed. Introducing M&Ms changed everything. I gave them a new context in which they were not threatened by new ideas and were willing to at least listen to them.

Maybe shocked is too strong a word, but giving them all M&Ms certainly surprised them. It got their attention and gave them a new way to think about evaluating new ideas. Change can be uncomfortable at first, but you can get used to anything if given enough time or the proper context. Note how we handled the change in the following story.

Points To Ponder From This Story:

1. **Sometimes, it takes shock treatment (or at least a surprise) to jump start change.**
2. **If you want people to be creative, *you the leader must first* be creative.**

Jury Duty

*D*avid Dykstra, Financial Controller for Armstrong International in Three Rivers called me one day. "I was just chosen for jury duty. The trial will last four weeks! The judge told me I was selected, partially because I could *afford* to serve four weeks since Armstrong pays its employees for jury duty."

"David, let me tell you a story about your brother Arlen, who was called in for jury duty. He was not paid the production bonus because the hours he spent on the jury were not considered *production* hours. Arlen knew the policy for production bonus could be improved. One day he stopped me in the shop and said, 'Armstrong is one of the few companies that pays its employees to be on jury duty. We get our full salary. But did you know that Armstrong doesn't pay the production bonus if I'm on jury duty? So, I still lose money.' We changed the policy after Arlen brought it to our attention. David, you go out and thank your brother. He saved you four weeks of lost production bonus!"

"It's too late. Arlen already told me the story."

David's moral: *If there's a way to do it better—find it.*—Thomas Edison

Changing in response to something that has already happened is reactive. Armstrong was proactive with its bonus program—long before profit sharing was invented. Armstrong's production bonus was born in 1907 as an incentive for regular attendance. It was an *attendance* bonus because it was common a century ago for workers to take a day off from work each week to go hunting or fishing to help keep food on the table. The first change came in the 1930s when it was changed to a *production* bonus. We rewarded workers for their performance. The more they shipped, while maintaining quality by using fewer hours, the better the bonus. Another change came in the 1970s when it became clear that employees were only taking vacations during the months when sales were poor and the bonus was small. This resulted in production problems because everybody took the same month off. We solved this by making it possible for those on vacation to be paid their production bonus. The third change came about as a result to the situation described in this story. Employees now get the bonus while fulfilling their civic duties on jury duty. We'll continue to change this program and any other to provide enjoyable experiences for our people.

Points To Ponder From This Story:

1. **If something is worth trying in the first place, it is worth changing to keep it relevant.**
2. **Change with the times or be left in the past.**

International Flags

How many of you have experienced seeing your country's flag while visiting another country? Remember how it made you feel? It was a familiar sight, a friendly sight and, for a brief moment, you felt like you were home. Then you probably felt proud and appreciated those who flew your country's flag. Armstrong International has always flown international flags for visiting guests from foreign lands, but we could only fly two flags. When we had more than two guests from foreign countries, we had to have little flags placed on the conference tables. That all changed one year at Armstrong International.

Just before Christmas of 1994, we installed seven flagpoles around the Armstrong logo. The Armstrong logo is found on a hill near the main road to Armstrong. What a beautiful sight these seven international flag are on windy days. We pointed lights at the flags so at night they would be seen. Every day we fly flags from countries where we have manufacturing plants, but when we have a visitor, we put up his or her country's flag. Immediately we began hearing, "Wow, I saw my country's flag. It made me feel good. I felt like I was home."

David's moral: *If you want to be an international company, think internationally.*

That familiar quote from Lao-Tze, the Chinese philosopher seems to fit here: "A journey of a thousand miles must begin with a single step." These flagpoles with their international flags are yet another step toward becoming a truly international company. We must think of our international customers. The problem is that we live in the United States, and we are used to dealing with American customers and their needs. I hope coming to work every day and seeing international flags will help our people to *change* and become more international aware.

To change our products to fit the needs of our international customers better, we must keep an open mind. The same can be said for service. Remember, it may be today in the United States, but it's tomorrow in the Far East. One morning Rex Cheskaty asked me how my day was going. Ok, but it's early, I responded. Remember,. David, 2/3rds of your empire has finished the day. Changing the hours we are open to improve service to international customers will only happen when we begin to think internationally. Change your time zone. Think in your customer's time zone.

With each passing day, more and more of Armstrong's customers are international. We began our change into an international company when we established representatives around the world to sell our products. We then built the Belgium plant in 1970. Since that time, we have entered into joint ventures in Japan, China and Australia. And we continue to look at opportunities in other countries. We do a very good job of servicing countries around the world. But we must continue to adapt and change our domestic policies, payment terms, pricing, product features and a thousand other things to continue on the path of becoming a truly international player. The international flags we see each day remind us to live, think and act like the international company we are.

Points To Ponder From This Story:

1. "A journey of a thousand miles begins with a single step."—Lao-Tze
2. "Change is a door that can only be opened from the inside."—an old French saying. How do we remember to open the door? By surrounding ourselves with little reminders – like international flags flapping in the wind.
3. It's a small world thanks to air travel, e-mail, the phone, video conferencing or overnight mail. But don't be fooled into believing that time zones, culture, language, and markets in other countries are the same as here in the good-old-USA.

Please Remember Me

"Have you heard . . . Brian Nimtz is leaving the company?"
"No way! I just talked to him yesterday. He seemed really happy with his job."

"That's what I thought!"

"Why is he leaving? Did they fire him or is he leaving on his own?"

"He's leaving on his own. He has a new job."

Later that day a call was made to Steve Gibson, Chief Financial Officer, who was Brian's boss. Brian told Steve that he was turning in his resignation. Brian offered to work until the end of the month, which Steve accepted. Steve then came to my office and told me the sad news. Both of us shook our heads in disbelief. Neither of us had seen this coming. What warning signs did we miss which would have alerted us that Brian was thinking about leaving?

David's moral: *The only constant is change.*

Change marches on. Depending on your point of view and situation, any given change may be good or bad, pleasant or difficult. So it is when, inevitably, employees leave. While I suppose some turnover is to be expected, at Armstrong we want to retain our employees as long as possible. So we stay alert to some of the signs that discontent may be setting in: loss of interest in work, closed door conversations, more time off than usual, increased sick days and less time spent with fellow workers. If an employee does decide to leave, don't forget the exit interview. It's an ideal time to learn something important—a lesson that may help you retain another valued employee in a different situation.

Points To Ponder From This Story:

1. **Your best employees are not looking for jobs, but they are being approached by other would-be employers.**
2. **Watch for the warning signs of a disinterested and disconnected employee.**
3. **Don't forget what you can learn from an exit interview.**

Let's Make a Promise to ...

"Promises we can begin keeping right here, right now." *David Armstrong*

- Deal with these facts realistically: Change is constant. Change is inevitable. Change is both good and bad.
- Remember that some things never change - like our core values.
- Become a change gourmet. Live to demo, prototype or experiment.
- Remember: our "attitude" towards change is all we can control.
- Manage change with integrity, honesty, and stay true to what we believe.
- Herd life; don't be stampeded by it.
- "Get used to being uncomfortable." Doug Bloss.
- Create an environment that *promotes* change. Use little reminders, like international flags.
- Think in our customers time zones, language, customs etc. Now act accordingly.

Chapter Twelve

Flying Slightly Out of Formation

Puts the same pieces together in a different way. Thinks out of the box. Sees things the rest of us can't. Marches to the tune of a different drummer. Thinks independently. Sees more levels than the rest of us. Thinks upside down. Thinks backwards. Is always a step ahead.

We've all heard these or similar descriptions in praise of those among us whose imagination and creativity make them different. A part of the group, they are nonetheless apart from the crowd. Maybe people say these things about you. The fact that a relatively few are singled out for this kind of description, points to a whole category of questions about creativity. Can we all be creative? Why are a few regarded so and most not? Are we born creative? Can we learn to be more creative through training and practice? And what difference does it make anyway?

In business it makes a great deal of difference. Creativity spawns innovations. Innovations become improved, differentiated products and processes that save lives, cut costs, save time, save energy, reduce pollution, cure disease, improve performance and on and on. And, of course, the companies who make the products delivering these consumer benefits have huge (and profitable) advantages in the marketplace. Could it be that the company that has a grasp on creativity also has a finger on the trigger of an idea machine that, properly nurtured and maintained, can produce innovations on a somewhat regular basis? If that is so, then shouldn't creating an environment where creative workers can flourish be pretty high on the priority list—at least of the same rank as production protocols, quality-control initiatives, performance reviews and policy manuals? It's one of my highest priorities. More of this later. But for now, let's get grounded on the basics.

What Is Creativity?

Linda Naiman, the founder of Creativity at Work™, defines creativity as the process of making new ideas into reality—in other words, making the products of imagination real. Like the tango, it takes two: The first is imagination or the thinking part—coming up with the idea. The second is the production part (innovation). So it follows that if you can imagine things but don't create innovations from them, you have imagination but not creativity. (1)

Could it be that the company that has a grasp on creativity also has a finger on the trigger of an idea machine that... can produce innovations on a somewhat regular basis?

I also like the definition offered by the United Kingdom's National Curriculum in Action. The authors of their National Advisory Committee's report published in 1999 takes a slightly different approach, but there are definite similarities with the definition we just saw. This definition also sees *imaginative* thinking or behavior as central to creativity. But it also suggests that the overall imaginative activity be *purposeful*, aimed at accomplishing a specific objective. In addition, the whole process must yield something *original* that has *value*. Although the concepts of originality and value are vulnerable to subjective judgments, it makes sense to me to include them. In reality, they would all seem to be part of the "production" part of creativity offered in Linda Naiman's definition. (2)

Can Creativity Be Learned?

According to a study cited by Creativity at Work™ maturation is one of the greatest threats to creativity. Naturally creative in the beginning, we slowly become uncreative as we come of age. (In response to a given situation, the average adult can muster perhaps half a dozen alternatives. Coming up with dozens, though, is nothing for kids.) Being creative is much like learning to play a sport. Practice is necessary to develop proper muscles. But just as important is an environment that supports practice, so the skill can develop and grow. And who creates this environment? You, the leader.

Teresa Amabile, head of the Entrepreneurial Management Unit at Harvard School of Business concludes after years of research on the subject that virtually any person of normal intelligence can do creative work. It depends on experience (knowledge, technical skill), talent (capacity to think in new ways and the perseverance to push through dry periods) and what she calls intrinsic motivation (being turned on by what you do). I love that! I'm always looking for my next fix at Armstrong. I'm always trying to outdo myself. Painted murals in the machine shop one day, crayons in the lobby the next. The idea that creativity is the exclusive property of so-called "creative types" is the first of several creative myths she outlines in a *Fast Company* Magazine feature in 2004. "The 6 Myths of Creativity" is the result of an eight-year study involving almost 12,000 individual diary entries from 138 employees assigned to creative projects in seven companies. The assignments included projects from consumer products, chemical and high-tech fields. Let's look at what Amabile believes creativity is *not*. It will give us a unique perspective on whether creativity can be a learned skill.

Myth 1: Only "creative types" can be creative. As we have seen, the facts— or probably the experience of most of us—just don't support this. Apparently, what's most important in work settings is a supportive environment and climate.

The more the members of a team are willing to share and openly debate ideas, the more creative they are.

Myth 2: Money spurs creativity. Surely, people need to feel appreciated and believe their compensation is fair, but most don't ponder it on a regular basis. If they do, it's a safe bet they're not being very creative. According to the research, some even see it as irrelevant. They regard fair compensation as a given.

Myth 3: Time pressure increases creativity. Although this was a common belief among the research subjects, the results showed the opposite. The researchers' conclusion? Creativity needs time to percolate and develop, and workers need time to engage a problem free from *all* distractions (not just the pressure of a short deadline).

Myth 4: Fear motivates creativity. Apparently, the world at large thinks fear and sadness stimulate creativity. In the research results, though, there was a positive link between creative ideas and feelings of joy and love and a negative association with anxiety, fear and anger. People are happiest on days when they nail a creative idea. But breakthroughs are most common if they were happy the *previous* day.

Myth 5. Competition is good for creativity. A lot of people believe that competition on the inside is a good way to speed up innovation on the outside. Amabile's team found just the opposite. Apparently, the more the members of a team are willing to share and openly debate ideas, the more creative they are. Competing for recognition and attention shuts down the flow of information. Collaboration beats competition hands down.

Myth 6. A lean organization is a creative one. Downsizing within an organization hits creativity hard. Communication and collaboration dry up. Fear of the unknown leads many to disconnect from the process.

Teresa Amabile's research has a lot to say about what creativity isn't. But the lessons about what it is and the parameters within which it flourishes are clear and present. Creativity is about people being allowed to fully engage the work they enjoy within an environment that recognizes and values it. (3)

I write stories about Armstrong heroes who show creativity. I spend money to support imaginative ideas like converting a conference room into Camelot. If I want Armstrong employees to use their imagination I must put my money and actions where my mouth is. I, the CEO of Armstrong, must blaze the trail by practicing visible imagination for all to see. If the leader is practicing creativity, others will feel comfortable doing the same. When that happens, good things are bound to happen.

Dream Up The Future

Japan's Nomura Research Institute lays out four stages of economic activity.

- Agricultural
- Industrial
- Informational
- Creative—constant innovation.

It's no wonder then, that when you log onto the Institute's Web site, the first thing you see is the line, "Dream up the future." This is the age of the thinker, creator, conceptualizer. The idea has enormous implications for business leaders. Success in the future may belong to those who will give new meaning to "thinking outside the box." Maybe tomorrow there will be no box. What then? In the years ahead it seems the stakes for man against white space will be higher than ever. Will creativity become the key differentiator for successful companies? Remember, innovation is imagination *plus* creativity or the coming to life of new ideas. Companies will need to produce something from all this thinking. What is this "something?" The National Innovation Initiative™ talks of it in terms of the social and economic value it will deliver. (4)

In 2006 IBM's Global CEO Study interviewed 765 CEOs from companies around the world and shared their views about agenda priorities in a report called "Expanding the Innovation Horizon." (5) The findings point to multiple venues for breaking new ground: Business Model Innovation, Operations Innovation and Products/Services/Markets Innovation. (6) In a 2005 feature, Business Week said the Knowledge Economy is giving way to what it called the Creativity Economy, and they used the special report ("Get Creative!") to launch a new online Innovation & Design portal.

Creativity is about people being allowed to fully engage work they enjoy within an environment that recognizes and values it.

From where I sit, making our companies more creative is beginning to sound like the number one job of business leaders. But only if we are the quickest, fastest and swiftest to market. Remember that chapter on urgency? What follows, it seems to me, is the need—NO, the necessity—for companies to train the microscope on themselves. How do we build a creative company? What kind of people work there? Maybe we should hire fiction authors instead of engineers. I'm serious! And how do companies of every stripe increase their creativity in a marketplace screaming for it? Maybe a place to start looking for answers is in the work of a Swedish researcher, Goran Ekvall, from two decades ago and the more recent refinements of investigators from the Center for Creative Studies at the State University of New York (SUNY)-Buffalo. Thanks to their work, you can assess your company's climate for innovation. They spell out nine distinct dimensions.

1. Challenge
2. Freedom
3. Idea Time
4. Idea Support
5. Trust and Openness
6. Playfulness and Humor
7. Conflicts
8. Debates
9. Risk-Taking

What Do Innovative Companies Look Like?

Perhaps even more important than assessing your company's *potential* for innovation by surveying its climate as we just did, is to take a long and hard look at exactly what innovative organizations look like and what they do. Fortunately, Ian Rose of Creativity at Work™ has already done this through his in-depth research within more than 700 companies around the globe, including Baxter, Ford, Rubbermaid, Saturn, Texas Instruments, Dow Chemical, DuPont and Xerox. So get out your paper and pencil and rate your company. According to this research, here are the primary attributes of innovative organizations:

Vision. This suggests a view toward long-term outcomes. Companies with vision can craft a future without the constraints of their past or present. Let me give you an all-too-common example. How many times have you and I heard, "David, things have been really great: don't screw things up by changing things." I hear this when Armstrong International is having a great year. We become trapped in our success. I've always believed it is easier to change a company when it's in trouble. This type of thinking traps us in the past or present.

The insight to change for the right reasons. This has to do with reinvention based on recognition of what the future will require. The short hand is: proactive not reactive. Such companies change because they see a better way, instead of being forced into change by circumstances.

This is the age of the thinker, creator, intrapreneur.

Open eyes. Innovative organizations are always looking to improve. They seek and listen to customers' feedback, using it to drive themselves into new areas, opportunities or challenges.

Substance over form. Innovative organizations allow new ideas to blossom and guard against the smothering effects of rule-making and review processes. Coming up with new ideas is more important than the processes which govern such brainstorming.

Creativity and innovation are built in, not added on. They start from the premise that everyone can be creative. They make heroes of creative problem solvers. Creative ideas do not frighten managers and leaders.

Organizational structures tend to be team-based. Teams underscore the idea that all participants can be creative—not just the top layers in a more traditional hierarchy.

Open communication rules the day. Information flows freely and knows no boundaries within the company. It accommodates individuality, minimizes red tape, promotes informal interaction and collaboration.

They don't take conflict personally. Conflict is not personalized. Spirited and intelligent dissent are valued and encouraged for they bring new, innovative ideas. Disagreement within the creative process tends to be about ideas not people.

They understand that who you know is important. This speaks to the importance of networking, relationships and collaboration.

They value diversity. Innovative organizations place value on individual differences and celebrate diversity in personality and cultural pedigrees. Looking for differences increases the possibility of novel connections. "Sticking out" is an okay thing.

They encourage fun at work. Engaged, inspired and empowered, people who have fun at work are more likely to buy in completely and participate fully, thereby increasing the potential of the creative process.

They believe in multiple answers. Innovative organizations do not commit to the pursuit of "the" idea. They leave their people open to wondering and pondering alternative ways of reaching solutions.

They encourage bending the rules. In such companies making waves is okay, rocking the boat is encouraged and management is brave enough to deal with the splash that "crazy" ideas sometimes make.

From where I sit, making our companies more creative is beginning to sound like the number one job of business leaders. But only if we are the quickest, fastest and swiftest to market.

They absorb errors and refuse to punish. Reasonable risk and probable false starts are part and parcel of the creative process. Innovative companies understand that employees will make mistakes and that not every creative start will end in a first-rate finish. By accepting failure as part of the process and not punishing employees for making mistakes, they keep the soil fertile and receptive for future seeds.

So how did you do? I'm happy to say that Armstrong fared pretty well. We're no 3M or Apple, but we hold our own. When I became CEO, I wanted to do something different from my father and grandfather. It was my responsibility to not only carry on what they had started, but to add to it as well. I decided that building a corporate culture that emphasized communication/management by storytelling, fun and creativity would be the best way to prepare Armstrong for success long after my leadership had ended. Here's a little of what we've accomplished.

Our Toilet Paper Secret

Has this ever happened to you? You've come up with an idea that you're really excited about. I mean really excited. But there's a problem. You can't get it approved. You try and you try to get people to support it, but no matter what you do, nobody gets behind it. Most of us, after a period of time, just stop trying.

But Rich Hitz is not like most people. Rich, the head of Research and Development (now President of Geo. B. Allan & Co.), figured out a way to use a revolutionary kind of steam trap on paper dryers. Rich knew his idea would work, but no matter what he did, he could never interest the President enough to take a look at his research, which proved the product would be a big seller.

Understanding that the President was very busy, Rich needed a creative way to grab his attention. He decided to write his report on a roll of toilet paper and sent it to his boss.

An interesting thing happened. The President read the report—and approved Rich's idea.

David's moral: *Consider the postage stamp. It sticks to one thing until it's done.*

No matter how good your idea is, it needs to inspire you if it is to succeed. And often this is the first step in inspiring others. If your idea is lost in the crowd, figure out a way to set it apart. If everyone is zigging, zag. Remember, there are relatively few ideas that sell themselves. So the next time you have a killer idea, don't let difficulty in selling it kill you. Find a way to get someone's attention. You may find that how you promote a good idea is just as creative as the idea itself.

Most of us will be positive and motivated when promoting our own ideas. When you pitch an idea to a superior, present it in a way that appeals to his/her self-interest. Self-interest is the best interest. While the next story doesn't deal with toilet paper, it does make use of some very provocative direct mail.

Points To Ponder From This Story:

1. Before you can inspire others you have to inspire yourself.
2. There are very few ideas that sell themselves.
3. Be creative in getting support like Rich Hitz was using toilet paper for his report.

Underwear

𝒯his story begins and ends when you receive a pair of men's underwear in the mail. Looking through the see-through plastic package you see white underwear and it's a size 34. "That's not my size." "I didn't order this." Then you notice printed on the plastic package in bold letters,

You're invited!

Armstrong-Hunt **"soft-ware"** Introduction

December 12th Chicago O'Hare Hilton

Bravo! Bravo to Doug Bloss, Corporate Vice President of Marketing and Sales, who boosted creativity that day.

David's moral: *When others zig, zag.*

Over the years, curiosity has claimed a lot of cats—and a good many recipients of clever direct mail packages. Getting underwear in the mail tends to pique your curiosity. Sure, underwear may offend a few, but the opportunity to win a lot of positive attention (and persuade them to attend) is too great to ignore. Are you brave enough to send undies in the mail? Why not? Set loose your imagination. It is one of the most underused assets of leaders. Go ahead, play it safe, or gain strength from knowing you will please many by being a creative leader.

Why be normal? An underwear mail delivery says, "I'm fun. I'm daring. I'm creative." What's more, this high-impact mailing had a very low-impact budget. I love it: Maximum attention. Minimum investment. If underwear in the mail says, "I'm fun," what's the message of the following story?

Points To Ponder From This Story:

1. **Nurture curiosity. Draw them in. Use any means possible - even underwear as a mailer.**
2. **Imagination will always offend the few but normally please the many.**
3. **You're not alone! There are many co-workers who are creative but unwilling to stand out for all to see. Be the first and get promoted.**

The Dugout

*I*n 1992 Armstrong International, Inc., Michigan, started changing its signs. *Conference Room A* and *Conference Room B* still hung above the doors in our basement. I sent a fax to Armstrong's executive staff offering two new names—The Sand Box and The Tree House. The next day I received a fax with their comments.

It read: "The staff went crazy about The Sand Box (sounds like a cat's litter box) and The Tree House (tree houses aren't in basements)."

Ahhh! I thought to myself. They just don't get it. It doesn't matter if a tree house is in the basement of the building. You're supposed to use your imagination.

These words were disappointing to me. I had been trying for so long to build the imagination of our people. I wanted to throw the fax away, but I read further.

"The staff would like to propose the following names: 1) The Dugout; 2) The Bunker; 3) The Clubhouse; 4) Future World; 5) Rathskeller; and 6) The Confessional."

Wow! I thought to myself, this is great. They're getting caught up in the spirit of using signs to promote an environment where fun and creativity can be the norm and not the exception. I phoned Rex Cheskaty, General Manager.

"Let's start with The Dugout. What do you think my next request is going to be?"

"You're going to want to decorate the rooms to match the names," Rex answered.

"You got it. Let's remember always to keep things simple and small so if it fails, we can go back to the way it was—quickly and with little expense."

Rex interrupts, "We thought you'd pick the dugout so we've already started decorating the room. We have some good ideas. Imagine, David, if you walk through the door and you immediately find yourself in a dugout. When you step out, you walk onto green AstroTurf with white lines drawn on it, representing a baseball diamond. On the one wall you will find 10 stadium seats, which we could use for training sessions. On the other wall might be a painted mural of the fans. Heck, they could be doing the wave. On the other wall you would have a bunch of lockers. And then, of course, you have the table shaped like a baseball bat where we have the meeting."

"Don't forget the peanuts and popcorn," I said. "We could leave baseball bats, gloves and balls lying around. And just imagine, if we wanted to recognize our partners, our customers, we wouldn't award them with a traditional plaque which everybody gives, but the game baseball autographed by the staff. Wouldn't that stand out when they took it back to their companies? Finally, we might want to put a big TV screen above the outfield like they do at the ball parks and use our CAD Solids Program to display new products to customers, or for slides and videotapes for training sessions. All these tools can be used to run our business and yet be fun and fit the atmosphere we are trying to create."

David's moral: *"If you want to make enemies, try to change something."* — Woodrow Wilson

I agree with Jack Welch of General Electric who believes that changes need to be big, powerful and revolutionary to overcome the bureaucracy. So dugouts, signs, storytelling and statues are just the beginning. They're all part of creating the Armstrong brand. So is using crayons.

Points To Ponder From This Story:

1. Imagine if...
2. "Ability may get you to the top, but it takes character to keep you there."—John Wooden, UCLA Coach.
3. If you are hiring somebody let them visit the dugout. I'll bet you hear, "I hope I get this job!"

Color Inside the Lines

The crayon fit tightly between the student's fingers as she began to press firmly on the paper. **Snap.** The crayon wiggles in her fingers but the crayon wrapper kept it together. Carefully she printed each letter of her name between the lines. With each letter the crayon grew weaker. There I'm done, as she checked the spelling of her name. Yep, S-Y-L-V-I-A in bright orange was correct. She handed the sheet of paper and box of crayons to the next student.

Duane carefully chose purple as his favorite color and began to print his name. Duane had trouble staying within the lines. He would obviously have to practice more. He then handed it to the next student.

"Here, Dave. Sign your name."

"Dave also grabbed a purple crayon and printed his first letter—D. Then he grabbed a green crayon and printed A and followed this with an orange V and another dark green E. He then chose purple for S, green for H, and when he was done, he had a rainbow of color spelling Dave Shutler. Several more students signed before the last student took the sheet of names back to the Armstrong University Professor.

"Here is the list with the names of those interested in dinner tonight."

"Thank you, students. Lesson one on creativity is done"

David's moral: *Smiling and laughing are free, easy to learn and require no experience.*

Everyone has been a seven-year-old. Let that child out again. Dave Shutler, who used all of the crayons in the box, did just that. Not bad for a former Colonel in the U. S. Air Force. Dave is also a lawyer and serves as the Director of Government Business for Armstrong Service government procurement. Dave used all of the crayons—a sign of a playful spirit and a creative soul. I'll bet Armstrong lawyers are more creative than the marketing people of many companies. Any takers?

According to Neil Postman, "Children enter school as question marks and leave as periods." Amen. Why is it that when we enter school, our creativity is high, we are full of ideas and nothing is impossible? By the time we graduate, we are unimaginative and straight-laced, whipped into conformity by years of rules about how to think, act, write and speak. We become this way because our teachers, adults, have forgotten how to be creative, too. Here's to bringing back the Tooth Fairy, leprechauns, Santa Claus, the Easter Bunny . . . and crayons.

Points To Ponder From This Story:

1. I have it on good authority you were all seven once.
2. "Children enter school as question marks and leave as periods."—Neil Postman

Let's Make a Promise to ...

"Promises we can begin keeping right here, right now." *David Armstrong*

- Give our employees a playground. Let them play.
- Imagine if... .
- Knock down fences and build bridges.
- Encourage daydreaming and hire fiction writers.
- Applaud risk-taking.
- Mix work and play.
- Communicate in every way and on every front possible.
- Remember there are no rules, policy or planned outcomes with imagination.
- Remember that imagination is one of the most underused assets of leaders.
- Inspire ourselves, then others.
- Be curious.
- Refuse to be normal. Remember, sticking out is okay.
- Remember that making waves is a must. Surf's up! Let's have fun.

Chapter Thirteen

Learning a New
Four-Letter Word

LEAD!! That's what I do nowadays. But there's no magic about it as far as I'm concerned. I lead as simply as I live. I'm a pretty straightforward kind of guy. I speak directly, communicate simply and try hard to always say what I mean and mean what I say. Of all the clichés that might be applied to an SOB (son of the boss) like me, this one probably fits best: "What you see is what you get." I'm not about trying to impress. I am what I am, and I'm confident that what I am will be enough to make me successful in whatever challenges I encounter. I know I can't lead *alone* and would never try. First, I need God's help. And second? I need the help of all the people who collectively make up Armstrong.

Not even for a nanosecond do I ever forget the privilege of my position. And I likewise never lose sight of the enormous responsibility I have to the Armstrong family and our extended family of employees, retirees, customers, suppliers, partners and friends. They call me leader, but my role is defined by those who follow. Together, we must uphold the Armstrong traditions. Protect the Armstrong brand. Preserve the Armstrong culture. And prepare for the Armstrong future. I have a big job, just as my father did before him and his father before him. But the name doesn't necessarily come with the nerve. Being an Armstrong doesn't guarantee an afterglow. I understood that I had a responsibility to earn our people's trust. Because without it, they would never follow me. Recognizing that and coming to grips with what it meant had a profound and humbling effect on me. I have become acutely aware of the magnitude of the gift I have inherited. Why? I'm surprised you ask, but perhaps it's a sign that this is a perfect place to revisit what Armstrong believes, how we operate and where we stand.

Core Values

At Armstrong, there is no such thing as situational ethics. Ours is one code of ethics that won't change by whim or the winds of chance. The translation is the same today as it was yesterday and will be tomorrow. We won't treat you badly because we're having a bad day or month or year. We'll do our best to deliver enjoyable experiences every day. If you're an employee or rep, bad things (violations of our core values) will get you fired. Good things will win you praise, promotion and our sincere gratitude. Shades of gray are for business suits and (unfortunately) the heads of senior statesmen, not standards of morality. At Armstrong, ethics come in two colors—black and white.

Armstrong believes in God, the power of prayer and the worth of every human being. We value dignity and integrity. We have unshakable faith in the simplest guide for conduct known to man: "Do unto others as you would have them do unto you." And we believe both the employee and the company have a crucial need to know themselves and each other and to live each day in accordance with these core values:

1. Faith in God, Family, Job (in this order)
2. Honesty
3. Fairness
4. Respect
5. Trust
6. Loyalty
7. Dignity
8. Hard Work
9. Kindness
10. Fearlessness

Furthermore, the mission of Armstrong is to be the simplest of the many companies with whom you may deal. Armstrong's old-fashioned values and integrity are meeting modern-day challenges and helping us live our vision of delivering enjoyable experiences to generations of global customers, employees, partners, neighbors and stockholders. Remember, what you see is what you get. This is Armstrong. You need to be okay with it because we're not going to change.

Armstrong believes in God, the power of prayer and the worth of every human being. We value dignity and integrity.

This, then, is what hangs in the balance. This is the huge responsibility I mentioned. I realized that if I didn't get this (my leadership) right, the indefinable spirit and force for good that infuse Armstrong and give it life, meaning and purpose, could be gone in a handful of years. That is very sobering. To assume leadership of a family-owned business is to bundle up its legacy and carry it on your back through thick and thin, into the middle of the great unknown future. So I didn't—and do not—take leadership lightly. I know I am the link between what was and what will be. I am no more or less important than those who shouldered this same task in other times. I am simply the most recent Armstrong to have arrived at this place.

The "L" Word

My style and much of what I believe about leadership grew out of the manner in which I was prepared to lead. In an effort to become well-rounded and develop a working knowledge about all aspects of our company, I traveled from department to department over a four-year period. I started in the factory, learning how the product was made. Then I made my way to production control, sales, purchasing, advertising and marketing. I understood the intent, but to this day I don't know whether it was a good idea or not.

It was good in that it gave me broad exposure to the departments of the company. But it was bad (or was it?) because the short exposure never really gave me a chance to get entirely familiar and comfortable in any role. The talk might have been that David didn't know what he was doing, and it was true! I'll be the first to admit that I never had the time with any given job to understand if fully and do it well. I could have had "Jack of all trades and master of none" tattooed on my forehead because for those four years that was my motto.

However, that constant state of instability and transition helped me develop an ability to live and function in chaos. Ever walk on a ship's deck in rough water? Well, it was kind of like that, and I got pretty good at it. I learned to walk upright without losing my balance, even when the floor was rocking. I got used to changing paces and changing places. As a result, I'm comfortable in such an environment today. So I think it's good that I learned this early on because a good many of the changes forced on us by globalization and technology keep things pretty well stirred up. I can deal effectively with them because they create situations that are familiar to me. Is it any wonder, then, that I like to keep my people slightly off balance? I think it's good for them because it helps prepare them for dealing with unexpected challenges. Life is unpredictable, and one of the best ways to leverage that fact to your advantage is to be able to move in sync with shifting players, circumstances and expectations.

I wanted to lead Armstrong by changing it, wanted our past to mentor our future but not predict it.

When I became a leader, I thought I had a pretty good understanding of the Armstrong brand. But I wasn't sure that others, both inside and outside our company, understood. Although I didn't necessarily see them this way (or this clearly) in the beginning, the challenges have become:

1. *Translating* what Armstrong means into a very tangible benefit that is universally recognized and understood
2. *Evolving* our corporate culture into an incubator to make creating and nurturing this benefit easier and more consistent
3. *Communicating* about all of this in a new and innovative way which would differentiate us

How to do this? I wanted to be more than a custodian of the Armstrong I had been handed. I wanted to lead Armstrong by changing it. I wanted our past to mentor our future but not predict it. Use what made us good in the past to make us great in the future. That was my plan. Now I say, "That was my plan," as if I had this all laid out ready to implement. That's not how it happened, as you might expect. It was more a process of trial and error, experimentation and discovery.

Each event or step gave context and a clearer meaning for each of those to follow. I honestly don't remember how it all fell into place and what the exact order of events was. That's not important. What is significant, I think, is the process—a chain reaction that continues today.

In some respects, crystallizing the ultimate Armstrong brand promise— enjoyable experiences—was the easy part. I can't quantify exactly how I got there or when. But the idea was a natural fit for our low-key style. A lot of companies talk about customer satisfaction, but I wanted to go beyond the endpoint of a sale. I wanted to suggest that the entire interface with any Armstrong product, service, facility, business unit or employee would be something to be warmly and fondly remembered. It would be enjoyable in whatever context was relevant and appropriate—a product that worked, a prompt refund, quick resolution of a miscommunication, a friendly voice on the phone, patient and courteous technical support.

Once the *enjoyable experiences* benefit was out there as a *promise* of what people could expect from Armstrong, it became instantly clear: Corporate culture and attitudes, as they existed then, needed to be better to support the promise. We were just not equipped to deliver every time we had an opportunity. To get there, we would have to create an environment where we created enjoyable experiences for ourselves and each other first. Were we having fun at work? Were we continually raising the bar for creativity, urgency, fun and intrapreneurship? This was the reason for and the beginning of a lot of the off-the-wall things I did at Armstrong. I wanted to lighten the place up and recast our attitudes about work and fun. How could we possibly make it clear to everyone that the job was never done until the customer had an enjoyable experience when we seldom had them within our own walls? I believed changing this was essential if our employees and business partners were to understand and accept that enjoyable experiences had become one of Armstrong's primary reasons for being.

I wanted to suggest that the entire interface with any Armstrong product, service, facility, business unit or employee would be something to be warmly and fondly remembered.

My seven S strategies became a way for employees to know how to deliver enjoyable experiences. Collectively, they are a blueprint for action. Yet they are deliberately so loosely defined and open-ended that any contributor can put a personal spin on them. You can't be in sync, in attitude and action, with the seven Ss and *not* deliver enjoyable experiences. It's this simple: If you're following these seven simple strategies, you're in sync with the Armstrong brand and customers are getting what we promise—enjoyable experiences.

Say These Three Times Fast

1. Swiftest
2. Simplest
3. Smallest
4. Spirit of Intrapreneurship
5. Surprise
6. Storytelling
7. Smiles

Swiftest doesn't mean *swift* - it means faster than swift. I want you to be the swiftest at whatever you do—generating a report, creating a new product, unloading a truck. Swiftest is all about having a sense of urgency, and urgency is about having and applying a can-do attitude. Please note that I didn't say swift or swifter but *swiftest*. If we are swift and someone else is swifter, that's not good enough. So we have to be the swiftest with nobody—but nobody—being quicker.

If you simplify, simplify, simplify, you will be the **simplest**. Don't complicate things. Find a way to simplify whatever task you face. And when you do, you'll find that you've become the *swiftest*, too.

Small is beautiful. People at Armstrong have heard me say that a million times. Be the **smallest**. Have the smallest budget. Don't assemble dozens of people and try to do a job on which no one can agree. Get two or three and get it done. Be the smallest.

If you work at Armstrong, I want you to act like you own the place! Think and act like an owner. Have a **spirit of intrapreneurship** in all that you do. ("Intra" being within or inside. So be an entrepreneur within your own department, group, function, etc.) If we keep our companies small in size, it helps create that entrepreneurial culture. So I strongly support breaking companies up when they get too big.

Sometimes the best part of delivering enjoyable experiences is watching the **surprise** on the faces of the recipients. When you exceed expectations, you surprise and delight. Always seek to surprise.

Communication through **storytelling** has become an Armstrong trademark. Tell stories to moisten dry information. Repeat stories to drive home your points. Look for stories. Become a story. Make storytelling a major part of your communications toolbox.

Can there be a more fundamental ingredient in the recipe for enjoyable experiences than **smiles**? Smiles disarm, soften, punctuate and are warm. Put a smile in your voice, too.

If you're following these seven simple strategies, you're in sync with the Armstrong brand and customers are getting what we promise—enjoyable experiences.

My search for how to improve communication at Armstrong led me to storytelling—almost by accident. (See Chapter One.) Storytelling was an answer to my prayers because it was a communications technique that functioned equally well on several levels. First, it is simple, familiar and effective. It is engaging and entertaining and rooted in a long tradition, having been practiced by generations of teachers and leaders in every culture throughout centuries of time. It amazed me that more companies were not using it to their advantage.

I realized storytelling was a perfect fit for my style and the objectives I had for Armstrong. In the process of simply telling stories about the life and times of Armstrong and our people, I found gold. Yes, storytelling was a creative way to reach people. But when I expanded my view and began to look at sharing stories as a whole new style of management and leadership, I saw the unmistakable glint of pure gold. Little did I know that my first four tentative stories told at Tom Peters' skunk camp were the leading edge of a huge wave of storytelling that would wash over corporate America. Now, more than a dozen years and five books later, I'm still telling stories. And I'm still amazed at what can happen when you tell good stories... like these.

One Hundred Dollars

𝒯his story begins with Willie Vedmore, Production Control Coordinator, driving to work one morning. It was going to be a nice day. The fog was burning off. The sun had already come up, and there were no clouds in the sky. Willie's eyes were focused on the road when he noticed a car parked on the side of the road. The car was old and in bad shape, and the hood was up, a sign of trouble. Standing by the hood was a young mother with her two children. She looked like she was in trouble, so Willie decided to pull over to see if he could help.

"Can I help you?"

"I don't know what's wrong. My car won't start. It just stopped when I was driving."

Willie approached the engine. "I don't know much about cars, but let me take a look. Maybe I can find what's wrong." While Willie was looking under the hood, Ron Schlesch, Vice President of Manufacturing for Armstrong, was driving by. Ron saw the young mother who looked like she was in trouble. He decided to pull over to see if he could help.

"Good morning. Can I help you?" asked Ron.

"That's okay. This man is trying to help me."

"Willie, is that you?" Willie poked his head out from behind the hood. "Hello, Mr. Schlesch. How are you?"

"Just fine. What's the problem?"

"I don't know. She said the car just stopped."

"Let me take a look." Very quickly Ron decided that the battery had shorted out. Ron reached into his back pocket, pulled out his wallet and gave Willie $100. "Here, Willie. Go down to the local auto store and buy her a new battery then give her the money left over for gas."

"Okay, Mr. Schlesch."

Ron walked back to his car, turned around to the young mother and said, "I hope you have a better day." He hopped in his car and drove off to work.

David's moral: *Kindness is greater than any V.P. title.*

As a leader, Ron made an impact on Willie that was still with him when he told me this story 20 years later. You never know what impact your words and deeds will have on people, on or off the job. Ron no doubt made quite an impact on the unnamed mother, too. To her, he was a dealer in hope. Willie got to see an entirely different side of his boss. It was obvious, Ron is a man who cares, who shows kindness to others. And most people will follow kindness.

Points To Ponder From This Story:

1. **A leader is a dealer in hope.**
2. **Look for the kindness in leaders. When found, remember it.**

Leaders Make Mistakes, Too

*A*rmstrong-Hunt in Milton, Florida, had received an order for copper coils that we knew would be tricky to produce. The work required intricate welding, and after we were finished, it was clear that job was not up to our standards. We were certain that it was just a matter of time before the welds would crack.

Chuck Rockwell, the General Foreman, knew there were two possible solutions. We could scrap the coils and start over. That would cost Armstrong about $2,000 in material alone, plus the labor costs on top of that. Our second option was to grind away the bad welds and try to salvage the job. Because Chuck had to pick me up at the airport, he left the decision up to his foreman. By the time Chuck and I got to the plant, the foreman and his welders had decided to scrap the product and start over.

"It's my fault we had this problem," Chuck told me in front of his staff. "I knew from past experience that welding copper is extremely difficult, but I didn't spend enough time with either our foreman or our welders to show them what needed to be done."

Chuck estimated that we could recover about $300 if the coils were sold for scrap. He decided to take the $300 and throw a party to celebrate his mistake because he was certain people would learn from it. From this day forward he knew we wouldn't undertake a new job until *everyone* understood what needed to be done. The employees would also learn that *everyone* makes mistakes, even the boss.

I am very proud of what Chuck did—for two reasons. In front of his co-workers and his boss (me), he took responsibility for making a mistake. And he decided to celebrate it. Here's an outstanding example of a leader who led by example. He said *publicly* it's okay to fail.

David's moral: *Be brave enough to fail as a leader.*

Although there seemed to be two options, there really was only one. Trying to patch up bad quality is simply not the Armstrong way. In the end, the foreman made the only decision he could, given that the company he worked for was Armstrong International. This little incident met the two criteria for reasonable failure—it taught us a valuable lesson and with the swiftest action we corrected the situation.

It's important to celebrate, or at least acknowledge, your mistakes publicly. Seeing is believing. Employees will actually generate more ideas when leaders demonstrate by their actions that they will support failure, especially when something is learned from it, as it was in this case. When people are freed from the fear of making mistakes, they are more eager to explore, invent and improvise. When they do so, they multiply their possibilities for innovation. If the boss can admit failure, then the troops feel more comfortable trying new ventures. And if it fails? Well, it happens now and again. Besides, the boss is not likely to get upset since he's failed, too.

This story was about a leader's bravery in the face of failure. The next one is not about failure, but it demonstrates how leaders have to be brave in other ways—how they need to be confident and secure, no matter what "others may think."

Points To Ponder From This Story:

1. Celebrate your mistakes—publicly.
2. Supporting failure does not mean supporting (or even tolerating) sloppiness.
3. Fail big. Significant gains come from significant failures.

Dull Crayons

*B*elieve it or not, our crayons have become dull. This happens because people use them to sign our guest register. The story I'm about to tell you begins at 108 Somogyi Court, South Plainfield, New Jersey. Dick Base was walking through the lobby one day when he noticed that the crayons all had dull tips. He picked up the box of crayons, turned it over and tried to sharpen a crayon. "Not good enough," Dick thought. He decided to go out and purchase a sharpener so he could sharpen them better.

That night he spent quite some time trying to find the perfect sharpener. Store after store he searched. The next morning Dick sat down in Everlasting Valve's lobby with the box of crayons on his lap and began sharpening. A few crayons later Don Richardson, Sales Coordinator, opened the door to the lobby. "Hi, Dick."

"Good morning, Don."

"What are you doing?"

"I'm sharpening crayons. I noticed yesterday that they were really dull, and it was difficult for our guests to sign in with them. So I decided to sit down and sharpen them."

"That's a good idea. They do look dull." Don left, and Dick continued sharpening his dull crayons.

David's moral: *Leaders who don't play are boring.*

Dick Base is the President of Everlasting Valve, so what's he doing sharpening crayons for crying out loud? Doesn't he have anything better to do? Oh, yes, I can almost read your mind on this one. But you see, it's not about wasting time, it's about *making* time for those intangibles I've spoken about. *Making* time for fun, the unexpected, the unpredictable. Any leader who does has to be confident in his approach and not be derailed by the criticism of others who are quick to judge. That's why Dick was working with crayons in the lobby, not in a back room behind a closed door. He knew what he was doing. More importantly, he knows who he is—a leader who is not afraid to walk close to the edge—in full view of everyone. Dick is not the only Armstrong leader with this kind of confidence. The next story will introduce you to Grant Kain.

Points To Ponder From This Story:

1. **He who is not willing to have fun is not ready to lead.**
2. **Leaders will always be vulnerable if they promote having fun at work.**

Kick Me!

This story recounts a time when Grant Kain, Plant Manager of Armstrong Machine Works, was having a bad day. It all started early one morning when Grant was talking with a machinist who had just produced some parts of bad quality.

"How could you run so may pieces of bad quality? Why didn't you catch the first couple of pieces?"

"It's not my fault, Grant. We're really busy."

Grant felt his anger rising and quietly he counted to himself: 1-2-3-4-5-6-7-8-9-10. Then he spoke, "Remember, you are to practice self-management and inspect your own quality."

"You're right, Grant. I'll do a better job next time."

The morning had grown only a few minutes older when Grant found himself talking to another machinist about bad quality. "Didn't you see the metal shavings in the casting?"

"No, sir. I don't know how I could have missed it, maybe it's because we are so busy."

Again, Grant could feel his anger growing, so he quietly counted to himself: 1-2-3-4-5-6-7-8-9-10. "You have time to clean the metal shaving out of the casting! It only takes a minute." Calmly, Grant walked away.

Only a few more minutes had passed and, just as Grant was to exit Plant One, a foreman stopped him. "Grant, one of the machinists just crashed one of our dies. The machine is going to be down for at least a couple of days." Grant slowly shook his head and then walked away in disgust. As he exited the building, he saw a metal bucket and without thinking he gave it a swift kick in anger. The bucket went rattling down the parking lot-clunk, clunk, clunk.

The morning was almost over when Grant found himself returning to Plant One. As he approached the door which he had left earlier in anger, he noticed the bucket placed back in its proper place. On the bucket was a happy face with the words . . . *Kick me*. Grant began to count to himself: 1-2-3-4-5-6-7-8-9-10.

David's moral: *"Acting in anger is like putting to sea in a storm."*—Benjamin Franklin.

Thomas Jefferson's counsel in matters of anger was, "When angry, count to ten before taking action; when very angry—100." Both Jefferson and Grant Kain knew not to take action when angry. Grant was not angry at the people who put the bucket back, making fun of him; he was angry at himself. Grant knew that as a leader he should not lose his temper. To keep his self-control, he would count to ten before speaking. Unfortunately, Grant failed to count to ten, and somebody had seen him kick the bucket.

"I left the bucket at the door with the happy face and the words *kick me* to help remind me to not lose my temper," said Grant. That's right, Grant told me this story. He wanted others to learn from his mistake. Now that's my kind of leader. Putting others ahead of himself. This bucket has been in the same place outside the tool room for several years as a constant reminder. It helps all of us remember the need to control anger.

Let's be real for a minute: As a leader, expect that your people will get angry with you on occasion. When it happens, let them vent. Hear them out—and really try to *listen* to what they're saying. Remain calm, but if the employee is out of control, get him out of the situation. That means sending him home to cool down and sort it out. Chances are good that he will be in to apologize and mend fences the next day.

Points To Ponder From This Story:

1. **Resist the temptation to blow up and let your temper get the best of you.**
2. **Leaders tell stories to remind us of what we learned.**

The Tin Box

Every Thursday, you'll see the General Manager or the Controller at Armstrong Machine Works walking around carrying a tin box. What's inside the box? Paychecks. Our paychecks are delivered in person week in and week out to everyone, whether they work in the shop or the office.

Since the General Manager or Controller is handing out those checks, he must know everybody's name. That's quite a feat when you consider this division has over 300 people.

Why do we do this? Because we want everybody to have a chance to be heard.

While we have an open door policy, not everybody feels comfortable walking into the corner office. By having an officer of the company hand out paychecks, everyone is assured that at least once a week, he'll have a chance to ask a question, voice a concern or suggest an idea to one of the people in charge.

David's moral: *"The secret to success is to do the common things uncommonly well."*—John D. Rockefeller, Jr.

"Make yourself available." It may be one of the best pieces of advice you could give any leader. Show by your presence you care. By handing out paychecks personally, we are, among other things, showing employees they are not numbers. We are saying they have names worth remembering and opinions worth hearing. Don't forget a note pad so you can take notes, so as not to forget the great ideas you might hear. In addition, taking notes reassures the employees you really care. But it's a two-way street. Don't just wait to be approached by someone with a question. Ask a few of your own opened-ended questions to draw people out: *What can we be doing better? How can we make Armstrong more fun for the customers and employees? What is the stupidest thing we do? What do you think of the new program we just put in place? What would you do today to help us be more urgent?* Don't ask for opinions and then not take lots of time to listen. When you have an answer always get back to the person. People yearn to be validated and made to feel worthy and important. Talking to them one-on-one is a great way to do so. And here's another one.

Points To Ponder From This Story:

1. Look for ways to show you care - like taking notes, listening for more than a few minutes, asking questions to clarify and returning with an answer.
2. Take the open door policy to the people and listen.
3. Spend lots of time with somebody when they want to talk. Giving your precious time says so much - mostly that you care and that they are important.

You're Promoted

*P*hil Long, President of Biggs-Gilmore Associates, the advertising agency we use, tells a story about promotions. Recently they had an opportunity to promote three people. It was decided that they would have a celebration honoring the promotions. A special lunch was to be catered. To top things off, the people who were to be promoted were told that their spouses would be attending the lunch when the promotions would be given. As the promotions were handed out, the spouses were there to share the moment with their loved ones. This only added to their enjoyment in receiving their promotions.

David's moral: *Promote a family, not just an employee.*

Promotions are special. Acknowledge that fact by making them so. Promote publicly. Promote where everyone can see. After all, it's better to *see* one promotion than to hear how to be promoted 100 times. Make sure everyone knows why the person is being promoted and, by all means, involve the spouse and children if possible. By the same token, make your hiring special. I heard that Ross Perot sends roses to the spouse of the person he just hired. What a great way to start a career with a company. Giving new employees and spouses a memorable first impression of your company will pay dividends for years.

Points To Ponder From This Story:

1. Make promotions special.
2. Making hiring someone memorable.
3. It's better to <u>see</u> one promotion than to hear **100** times how to be promoted.

Let's Make a Promise to ...

"Promises we can begin keeping right here, right now." *David Armstrong*

- Seek God's help in our leadership.
- Respect, remember and learn from those who came before us.
- Protect and defend our core values. At all times! At all cost!
- Simplify... and don't forget the other Armstrong seven S's.
- Remember that Armstrong's primary reason for existence is to provide *enjoyable experiences.* What's yours?
- Get comfortable with instability.
- Become the champion and guardian of our corporate culture.
- Never rest until we have delivered an enjoyable experience.
- Ask every employee to think and act like an owner.
- Become a story worth telling.
- Don't hide our failures, put a spotlight on them.
- Make ourselves available. Don't hide behind the open door policy.
- Show we care over and over and over.
- Don't assume, ask.

David Armstrong

Chapter Fourteen

Short Stories. Long Odds.

What were the odds that a longish-haired, 30-something corporate executive would attract the attention of high-powered, hardwired CEOs representing a cross section of American business? Never mind that I was the COO of Armstrong International, Inc., a family-owned global manufacturer with locations in the United States, Canada, Europe and the Far East.

It was November, 1989, and the scene was a classroom overlooking the dunes at Palo Alto, CA., site of a Master Skunk Camp run by Tom Peters. It was a follow-up to Tom's previous five-day camp. This time each participant was asked to bring three persons from his company. I invited Doug Bloss, Vice President of Sales, Tom Morris, General Counsel and Steve Gibson, CFO, to come along.

During a Bragging Rights session, each of the original participants had 10 minutes to showcase how they had applied what they had learned in the original session. No holds barred. We all wanted to impress each other—especially Tom Peters. The room looked like a staging area for a Ringling Brothers parade. One guy was dressed in a skunk outfit. Others had loads of equipment, displays and assorted paraphernalia.

I brought in four sheets of paper.

As I started my presentation, my guys sank lower and lower into their seats, trying their best to be invisible. This was going to be bad. On each of the four sheets of paper was a story—a simple narrative about the life and times of Armstrong, its people and its business. When I finished the last story, the wave of questions swelled and washed over me. They continued right up until our break time.

Sometime during all of that, Tom Peters passed me a sheet on which he had doodled a couple of stick figure men carrying brief cases with the title, "Managing

By Storying Around." At the bottom was "To David Armstrong, first ever MBSA Award." Although "Managing By Storying Around" *did* become the title of my first book, when Doubleday called a week later, I had to ask in all honesty, "What book?"

That Was Then. This Is Now.

The Airstream travel trailer with its sleek silver trademark finish looks like any other—except for the bold orange letters that march across its side. They read StoryCorps. As I write this, the trailer sits in the middle of Bronson Park in Kalamazoo, Michigan, about 25 miles north of the Armstrong International campus in Three Rivers, Michigan.

The trailer is a StoryCorps Mobile Storybooth, and its mission is to capture the extraordinary stories of not-so-ordinary Americans from all walks of life. StoryCorps (www.storycorps.net) began in 2003 with the vision of inspiring ordinary citizens to record their stories in sound.

For a nominal charge, which can be waived if necessary, Americans can become a part of history. At permanent StoryBooths or at mobile units that tour the country, people can conduct broadcast-quality oral history interviews with the guidance of a trained facilitator. At the end of a typical 40-minute session, participants walk away with a CD of their interview. With their permission, a second copy will become a permanent part of the American Folklife Center's archives at the Library of Congress. The material is accessible to the public at the American Folklife Center and on the Library's Web site at www.loc.gov. Selected segments may also be aired on public radio or be compiled onto "Best of StoryCorps" CDs.

In a flash, I understood that people liked stories and will listen to them.

The National Storytelling Network (www.storynet.org) focuses on the role of storytelling as a unique performance genre, a powerful teaching aid and a cultural transformation technique. In 1973 Jimmy Neil Smith created the National Storytelling Festival when 60 people showed up to hear a few Appalachian tales from the back of a hay wagon pulled up beside the town courthouse. In the decades to follow, the number has grown to 10,000 and the hay wagon has been replaced with large, circus-like tents sprinkled throughout the town of Jonesborough, Tennessee.

Storytelling Is Alive And Well.

When I first started using storytelling as a deliberate leadership technique at Armstrong International, Inc. nearly two decades ago, I was amazed that more business leaders weren't doing the same. Every company had people and therefore stories. So why weren't they taking advantage of them?

The more I read about corporate and organizational culture, the more I became aware that storytelling is alive and well in every company. While it may not be recognized and leveraged as a formal management or leadership tool, it thrives nonetheless.

Thanks to storytelling, our people have a very clear understanding of what Armstrong stands for and what we won't stand for.

In *Corporate Cultures: The Rites and Rituals of Corporate Life*, Terrence Deal and Allan Kennedy explain that storytelling is part of a vital *hidden hierarchy* which looks and functions far differently than the formal organizational chart. This hidden hierarchy has "other jobs" performed by storytellers and a host of other unofficial but powerful functions. Together, they make up what Deal and Kennedy call the "cultural network."

In the mid-1980s there were few corporate leaders who had deliberately and publicly embraced storytelling as a leadership style. As word spread, I had speaking engagements. I gave numerous interviews for magazine articles and I appeared on radio and television. In addition, the Armstrong brand of storytelling was featured in several books, including *Credibility* by James M. Kouzes and Barry Posner, *The Pursuit of Wow!* by Tom Peters, Evelyn Clark's *Around the Corporate Campfire* and *The Leadership Genius of George Bush* by Carolyn Thompson and James Ware. Today, there are a growing number of corporate executives who tell stories, and I asked Evelyn Clark, "The Corporate Storyteller," why.

"Since I began working with corporate storytelling in the early 90s... it's been perplexing to me that so few companies have recognized and leveraged the power and value of storytelling, particularly because the power and value were so obvious to me—and storytelling for business clearly intrigued nearly everyone I spoke to. But while everyone seemed to find it an engaging idea, more often than not, they didn't find it of enough value to learn about applying it in their organizations—until the past few years.

Since the turn of the 20th Century, our culture has primarily valued scientific findings and financial data (the products of left-brain activity), and business was driven by manufacturing, which requires left-brain skills. As a result, CEOs have traditionally come from the operations side of the enterprise, mostly from finance and sales.

Also, it's much easier to see the value of hard-data skills because it's easy to draw a direct path to the bottom line. Because hard-data skills have been held up as the 'gold standard' of success, right-brain activities, such as creativity, intuition and emotion have not been considered valuable.

Since it falls in the 'soft skills' category, storytelling has not been seen as a worthy effort in business until fairly recently. Now that the economy is increasingly service-based and truly global, building relationships has become essential. The need to build mutually beneficial relationships, in turn, created high demand for 'soft skills,' such as cross-cultural manners and effective communication, which, of course, includes storytelling."

The more I read about corporate and organizational culture, the more I became aware that storytelling is alive and well in every company.

"I also agree with the premise that as our dependence on high tech increases, our need for the personal touch grows—and storytelling fills that need in many ways: creating community, building dreams, reaching customers' hearts, enhancing understanding and capturing knowledge stored in employees' brains."

In addition, storytelling is a more clearly visible and viable part of popular culture. There is growing interest in storytelling as performance and as a form of practical communication. Visibility of and support for initiatives such as the StoryCorps and the Storytelling Network are evidence that more and more people are recognizing the power of the simple request: "Let me tell you a story."

Help For Storytellers

The growing recognition of storytelling's latent power in business has led to considerable help for businesses who want to leverage storytelling. Companies like McLellan Wyatt Digital and The History Factory help companies plan and manage the collective assets that are their history. Help in developing "narrative strategies" is available as is training and coaching for "organizational storytelling."

Evelyn Clark (www.corpstory.com) calls herself The Corporate Storyteller. Evelyn is a veteran of corporate stories, and she works with leaders and work teams who want to develop their most powerful stories and tell them more effectively. She helps leaders to inspire and sustain success by conducting customized workshops, facilitating retreats, creating communication plans, developing core stories and providing a variety of other services.

So you see, becoming a successful business storyteller is easier now than it has ever been. You have always had the raw material. In fact, it's all around you. Just listen! Check your e-mail for the stories that might lie hidden there, talk to retirees about long-forgotten stories and look for new items or things out of place which provoke the question: *Is there a story here?* Find them in the eyes and on the faces of the employees who come through the front door every day. Delve into employees' memories and ask about the simple objects that adorn their work stations.

But does storytelling really work? My answer would be a resounding, probably deafening, YES! Storytelling is a versatile leadership tool, and I've seen it work its magic on Armstrong employees around the world. But don't take my word for it.

Evelyn Clark works with lots of companies who think it works: Microsoft, World Vision, VeriSign, State Farm Insurance and Costco Wholesale, to name a few. And when it comes to Nike's colorful history, their mandate could easily be, "Just tell it."

After all, Nike has integrated storytelling into its corporate life. The message they seem to be sending is that a prosperous future rests squarely on an understanding of the past. So newcomers learn about a retired track coach, experiments with rubber and a family waffle iron, the death of a runner who campaigned for better equipment and selling footwear out of a car. Why? Because knowing such things is essential to connecting with Nike and understanding how they became who they are.

What's more, the stories don't stop with Nike employees. They're drilled down to the legions of salespersons who punch the registers at The Athlete's Foot and Foot Locker outlets as well as other larger retailers carrying Nike products.

Voice Mail

It all started with, "I'm sorry; I am not in the office right now. Please leave a message after the tone and I will return your call." The real tragedy in this story was that I had heard the same message six times in a row while trying to find a live body to talk to! Now, I must admit that a few times I pushed the "O" on the phone pad to get the switchboard. At this point I would get a live operator and each time I was transferred, I heard the message, "I'm sorry, I am not in the office right now. Please leave a message after the tone and I will return your call."

A few days later I found myself in Belgium preparing to celebrate the 30th anniversary of Armstrong International in Belgium. Ron Schlesch had been in Belgium for a few days and had tried to make calls to Armstrong in Michigan. Ron told me that all he was getting was voice mail. He couldn't get anybody to answer the phone. Roger Clossett overheard our conversation and added, "Me too!"

David's moral: *Voice mail will kill your credibility one message at a time.*

Okay, I'm not an idiot. Voice mail has its place. It can be a good and practical thing. And, in reality, I can see how it could make responsible people more productive and effective (if they actually follow up on messages they would otherwise have missed). But I'm also human, and I know employees may hide behind voice mail, using it as a shield to protect them from interruptions while working on a project or taking a break. It's also a dandy device for putting people off when it's close to lunch or quitting time.

But hello, people. Can't you see that every company needs to keep the human touch alive and well? We need it to make customers feel welcome and unique. Nowadays, getting a live person is special. You think you've won the Lotto.

Remember, a live voice says, "I care. I'm eager to treat you like a person," and "You are important to me."

A live voice is mightier than any pen, e-mail or voice mail. The human voice builds personal relationships. A live person draws out more knowledge from a customer. With voice mail no questions can be asked, no explanations given, no clarification can be sought about what is possible or available. People—not answering machines—sell products, services, comfort, peace of mind and confidence. And don't we all want to deal with humans rather than machines? The next story deals with a different but related telephone problem.

Points To Ponder From This Story:

1. **A company is known by the way it answers its phones. And it all starts with a living breathing person.**
2. **Voice mail does not kill; it permits suicide.**

Three Telephone Rings

" Let it be known that I, David Armstrong, count how many times your telephone rings." I spoke these words many years ago. I remember saying, "Don't you just hate it when you call someone and the phone rings and rings and rings? No one answers it. It's a sign of rudeness. Think how it makes Armstrong look to the customer who is calling. We are going to be different here at Armstrong. We will answer our phone in three rings. This will knock our customers' socks off, not to mention each other's. It will get us in the habit of promoting urgency—urgency in answering the phone. If you are talking with somebody, even me, I still want you to answer the phone in three rings. If you do not answer the phone, then please have someone assigned to pick it up within three rings. I'll be counting."

Several months passed. The people had not taken me seriously. I asked the switchboard to start counting the number of rings by person. They kept a log sheet for me. It was amazing. The same people were the abusers. Sometimes the phone would ring as many as eight or nine times. Sometimes it would never get picked up. I started taking this weekly log sheet to each of the people and told them that we were counting how many times their phone rang. We knew they were not answering the phone. Boy, were they shocked! Again, I repeated my message on the importance of answering the phone. I am happy to say that after a year of following up, the phones starting getting answered within three rings by everyone at Armstrong International.

Four years later, our order backlog was three times higher than normal, international orders were up 82%, we installed a new computer system, we made major moves of machinery in the shop that disrupted our production and we installed a new manufacturing system which we call AMPS. Boy, were we busy! (For the past year, I have been tolerant of the phone ringing more than three times due to the workload and stress. Now, with things back to normal, it is time for the phone to be answered within three rings. I'll be counting.)

David's moral: *A company is known by the way it answers its phones.*

Remember those "thousand little things" that improve quality I talked about? Well, telephone habits would certainly qualify. But I'm not so sure I would put them among "little" things. It is certainly true that a company is known by the way it answers its telephones. Think about it: When you're calling someone, a quick, enthusiastic response speaks volumes. We just read about all the things a live voice communicates.

The words used in answering your phones may be pleasant enough, but unless they're backed up with a *positive* attitude and a cheerful voice the opportunity to *wow* the customer is lost. And claiming you're too busy doesn't cut it either. It's just another symptom of an attitude in need of an adjustment, if not a complete overhaul. How can employees of any business be too busy to serve customers? I don't get it.

"My greatest concern is not whether you have failed," said Abraham Lincoln, "but whether you are content with your failure." It seems to fit this discussion. Failing to answer a phone promptly is concern enough. But to <u>not</u> be concerned about this failure or to not see its dangerous tendencies? That, my friends, is more than I can take. Not picking up such subtleties on your radar is the first step toward mediocrity. But not at Armstrong. We will not be like other companies. We will answer our phones in three rings. Count on it... because I am. Literally.

Points To Ponder From This Story:

1. Answering the telephone within three rings has become an Armstrong tradition.
2. Justifying a fault doubles the mistake already made. You're not too busy to answer the phone in three rings every time.
3. "Everybody does it," doesn't make it right. We are Armstrong International, Inc.

Slam

*J*ust the other day a tremendous bang echoed through my ear as someone slammed the phone down onto its cradle. It happened after our conversation had ended. My immediate thought was "How rude!" Then I thought maybe this person couldn't wait to hang up because they didn't want to talk to me. This told me that there is an Armstrong employee who doesn't want to talk to the Chief Storytelling Officer (for the more traditional among you, Chief Operating Officer) of their company. If they're foolish enough to do it to me, they'll do it to everyone. And you who slammed the phone down on me, read the following to improve your telephone skills. You know who you are.

David's moral: *On the phone as in person, courtesy counts.*

Hearing a phone being slammed down is a little like having the caller yell, *I'm too busy for you.* It's rude and conveys that the caller doesn't want to talk to you which is unacceptable. I don't like it, and I don't think you do either. It's an insult and indefensible. Enough said.

Points To Ponder From This Story:

1. Telephone lines are a company's life lines.
2. Wait a few seconds after you say "goodbye" before you hang up. Make it a new habit and you will never need to worry if you hang up on your boss.

Hello!

"**H**ello—Tom Henry speaking."

That's what you will hear when you call Tom Henry, Sales Manager at Armstrong Petro/Chem, Michigan. If you've ever heard Tom Henry's hello, you will know what I mean when I say it's full of energy, passion and excitement. Tom sounds like he's having fun at work. Tom sounds like he's happy to speak to you. I for one am going to try to answer the phone more like Tom because I too enjoy my work and want the people who call me to have their spirits lifted.

David's moral: *Keep your eyes on the things you cannot see.*—Confucius

What's better than answering your telephone in three rings? Answering it within three rings with excitement, energy and a smile in your voice. Yes, it may be tried and true, but it's still worth repeating: It's not what you say but *how* you say it. Passion, excitement and eagerness in your voice will speak more loudly and communicate more clearly than the words you speak.

Tom Henry creates an image by how he answers his phone. You can do the same. Create a picture of a "can do" go-getter for the person on the other end of the line. Don't be hokey, but imaginative . . . like the caller in this last story.

Points To Ponder From This Story:

1. Answer with excitement in your voice. Become an entertainer. You want the caller to have an Enjoyable Experience while talking with you. She/he should hang up only to be anxious to call you again.
2. It's not what you say, but how you say it.
3. You create your own personal image by the way you answer your phone.

Man's Best Friend

"**H**ello, this is Dr. Smith, the veterinarian for Mischa, and this message is for Mischa. The pathology report came back and confirmed what I suspected. We do have a hormonal imbalance. The pathologist has ruled out all the other skin diseases. It points toward the abnormality of the sex hormones, and we will be doing our blood tests next month to confirm this. Have your parents practice catching a urine sample by walking around with a small cup and bending down and catching the sample—do a lot of practice runs, because on the day of your next visit I would like to have another urine sample. The sample that we looked at during your first visit was a very small sample, but it showed a lot of protein. I just want to make sure that there are no other problems going on in your urinary tract, which could spell other worries for us. Come in for your next visit with an empty stomach and have your parents bring a urine sample. If you have any questions, call me back.

David's moral: *Creativity adds impact to your communications.*

This message was memorable for more than one reason. First of all, Dr. Smith himself called. He didn't leave it to an underling. That made an impact on us. Of course, the tongue-in-cheek way he left the message "for Mischa" was clever and entertaining. The good doctor managed to give Mischa's "parents" all the information we needed, and he did so in a whimsical way which eased our minds and put us at ease. Well done, Doc.

Points To Ponder From This Story:

1. The secret of genius is to carry the spirit of a child to work.
2. Customers for life - no matter what the price.

Let's Make a Promise to …

"Promises we can begin keeping right here, right now." David Armstrong

- Tell stories because storytelling works. People listen, learn and remember.
- Inject passion into our business through storytelling.
- Make great stories our company's best ambassadors.
- Believe storytelling is timeless.
- Use the treasure of stories our company, any company, has.
- Tell stories to become more effective leaders. It's all about communication.
- Tell stories to make a point.
- Tell stories to teach a lesson. Don't forget those morals.
- Tell stories to recruit and train.
- Use stories to empower our people.
- Use stories to offer recognition and as a reward to our employees.
- Use stories to help sell products, services and the very image of our company.
- Keep the human voice alive and well for our customers.
- Answer our telephones within three rings.
- Communicate energy and eagerness by putting passion into our voices.
- Communicate with imagination and creativity.

References

Chapter Two
1. http://www.ethics.org/research/2005-press-release.asp
2. http://www.business-ethics.com

Chapter Three
1. 1 http://www.google.com/intl/en/about.html
2. http:// www.netflix.com
3. htpp:// www.southwest.com/about_swa/press/factsheet.html
4. Freigberg, Kevin and Jackie Freiberg, Nuts! (New York: Broadway Books 1989), 19

Chapter Four
1. Holland, Angus and Emily Ross. *100 Great Businesses and the Minds Behind Them.* (Naperville, Illinois: Sourcebooks, Inc., 2004), 159-163.
2. Id at 201-205.
3. Covey, Steven. *The Seven Habits of Highly Effective People.* (New York: Simon & Shuster, 1989), 71.
4,5,6. http://www.ebri.org

Chapter Five
1. http://www.southwest.com
2. http://www.valvoline.com/carcare (Search for "Lemon Laws.")
3, 4, 5. http://www.jdpower.com/corporate/news/releases (Search for "Vehicle Dependability Study" and Retail Banking Satisfaction Study" by year.)
6. http://www.consumeraffairs.com/news04/2007/05/fda_broken.html (Use Search Function and search for "FDA Broken.")
7, 8. http://www.worldbank.org/mdf1/battling.htm
9. http://www.mackinac.org/article.aspx?ID=6954
10 http://www.abcnews.go.com/2020/Stossel/Story?id_1500338 (Search for "Jan. 13, 2006 Stupid in America.")

Chapter Six
1. 1.http://www.money.cnn.com/2007/01/16/news/companies/faithfriendly_companies.fort u en/index (Use Search Function for Fortune and search for Marc Gunther, Finding God at work.)
2. http://www.cbsnews.com/stories/2007/04/19/earlyshow/main2707047.shtml
3. http://www.nd.edu/~cba/011221/press/2005/05_enderle-faith_business.shtml

4. http://www.usnews.com/usnews/biztecharticles/050131eechaplain.htm

Chapter Seven
1. Holland, Angus and Emily Ross, *100 Great Businesses and the Minds Behind Them* (Naperville, Illinois: Sourcebooks, Inc. 2004), 190-195.
2. 2 Ibid.
3. http://abcnews.go.com/GMA/Technology/Story?id=3179394&page=1
4. http://www.theacsi.org (Search News section for 2007 news releases of February 20 and May 15.)

Chapter Eight
1. http://www.scifi.com/sfw/issue92/classic/html
2. http://www.americanwest.com/trails/pages/ponyexp1/.htm
3. http://pws.prserv.net/sadowsky/papers/pakistan97.pdf
4. http://www.sharpened.net/glossary/definition.php?yottabyte
5. http://www.usabilityviews.com/uv007462.html
6. http://www.yaleglobal.yale.edu/display.article?id=3653
7. http://www.en.wikipedia.org/wiki/Globalization
8. http://www.theglobalist.com/DBWeb/StoryID.aspx?StoryId=4527

Chapter Nine
1. Angus, Holland and Emily Ross, *100 Great Businesses and the Minds Behind Them* (Naperville, Illinois: Sourcebooks, Inc., 2004), 38-40.
2. Id. at 59-63.
3. Freiberg, Jackie and Kevin Freiberg, *Nuts!* (New York: Broadway Books, 1998)
4. Angus, Holland and Emily Ross, *100 Great Businesses and the Minds Behind Them* (Naperville, Illinois: Sourcebooks, Inc., 2004), 9-14.
5. http://hbswk.hbs.edu/item/3807.html
6. http://www.cnnmoney.com Use the Search function, searching for "A Startup's Best Friend? Failure"
7. http://www.nfib.com/object/IO_27577.html
8. Freiberg, Jackie and Kevin Freiberg, *Nuts!* (New York: Broadway Books, 1998), 128-134.

Chapter Ten
1. http://www.8minutedating.com/howItWorks.shtml
2. Angus, Holland and Emily Ross, *100 Great Businesses and the Minds Behind Them* (Naperville, Illinois: Sourcebooks, Inc., 2004), 323-328.
3. http://www.google.com/corporate/history.html

Chapter Eleven
1. http://en.wikipedia.org/wiki/Countries_affected_by_the_2004_Indian_Ocean_earthquake
2. http://nymag.com/news/articles/wtc/1year/numbers.htm
3. http://www.npr.org/templates/story/story.php?storyId=4585992

References

4. http://inventors.about.com/library/weekly/aa120198.htm
5. http://news.com.com/2100-1040-940713.html

Chapter 12
1,4,5. http://www.creativityatwork.com
2.   http://www.ncaction.org.uk/creativity/whatis.htm. Use Search function and search for What is Creativity?"
3. http://www.fastcompany.com/magazine/89/creativity.html
6. http://www.businessweek.com/magazine/content/05_31/b3945401.htm

David Armstrong

Some of the stories in this book were taken from:

David Armstrong

Index